I HATE EVERYONE . . .

I HATE EVERYONE . . .

JOAN RIVERS

STARTING WITH ME

BERKLEY BOOKS, NEW YORK

THE BERKLEY PUBLISHING GROUP
Published by the Penguin Group
Penguin Group (USA) Inc.
375 Hudson Street, New York, New York 10014, USA
Penguin Group (Canada), 90 Eglinton Avenue East, Suite 700, Toronto, Ontario
M4P 2Y3, Canada (a division of Pearson Penguin Canada Inc.) • Penguin Books
Ltd., 80 Strand, London WC2R 0RL, England • Penguin Group Ireland, 25 St.
Stephen's Green, Dublin 2, Ireland (a division of Penguin Books Ltd.) • Penguin
Group (Australia), 250 Camberwell Road, Camberwell, Victoria 3124, Australia
(a division of Pearson Australia Group Pty. Ltd.) • Penguin Books India Pvt.
Ltd., 11 Community Centre, Panchsheel Park, New Delhi—110 017, India •
Penguin Group (NZ), 67 Apollo Drive, Rosedale, Auckland 0632, New Zealand
(a division of Pearson New Zealand Ltd.) • Penguin Books (South Africa) (Pty.)
Ltd., 24 Sturdee Avenue, Rosebank, Johannesburg 2196, South Africa

Penguin Books Ltd., Registered Offices: 80 Strand, London WC2R 0RL, England

This book is an original publication of The Berkley Publishing Group.

I HATE EVERYONE . . . STARTING WITH ME

FIRST EDITION: June 2012

Library of Congress Cataloging-in-Publication Data

Rivers, Joan.
I hate everyone . . . starting with me / Joan Rivers.
p. cm.
ISBN 978-0-425-24830-0 (hardback)
1. Misanthropy—Humor. I. Title.
PN6231.M59R58 2012
814' .54—dc23
2012008413

PRINTED IN THE UNITED STATES OF AMERICA

10 9 8 7 6 5 4 3 2 1

The suits at Penguin have asked/suggested/demanded that I point out to everyone (especially litigious crackpots and humorless celebrities) that I'm a comedian and this is a humor book and if you're too dumb/stupid/feebleminded to figure that out, then that's *your* problem.

Why they asked/suggested/demanded that I do this, I don't know; nothing in this book is actionable because (like politicians, clergymen and Mel Gibson) every word of it was spoken to me directly by God.

—Joan Rivers

FYI: God called collect. What a cheapo.

To

The Son of Sam, David Berkowitz.
Call me.

and

O.J. Simpson, who deserves another chance.
Maybe the lippy ex-wife had it coming.*

* I'll bet you thought I was going to dedicate this to Melissa and Cooper. Well, you thought wrong.

I hate authors who thank, honor or acknowledge everyone they've ever met for "helping me, in some big or small way, to travel on this journey I call life, and have made me the person—and author—I am today."

Fuck them! Since the day my mother bought me at the auction, I've had nobody to thank or acknowledge. And if anyone says I do, I especially hate them.

CONTENTS

I HATE EVERYONE . . .

How do I love thee? Let me count the ways.

—ELIZABETH BARRETT BROWNING, 1850

How do I hate thee?
How much time do you have?

—JOAN RIVERS, TODAY, ABOUT TWO-ISH

■

Love may be a many-splendored thing, but hate makes the world go round. If you think I'm kidding, just watch the six o'clock news. The first twenty-nine minutes are all about dictators and murderers and terrorists and maniacs and, worst of all, *real housewives*. And then, at the very end of the show, there's a thirty second human-interest story about some schmuck who married his cat. I rest my case.

Some things I've hated forever, some are new acquisitions and some are just passing fancies. Today I hate: happy TV weathermen, feminists who believe Gloria Steinem's great looks hurt her, Gloria Steinem herself, people who mispronounce the word *ask*, studio apartments, guidance counselors, first ladies, old people. So if any of this offends you, or you happen to love puppies and kittens and the infirm . . . well . . . I'm impressed. I hate you, but I'm impressed . . .

I know what you're thinking: "Joan, hate is a very strong word." You're right, it is, but I use it as an umbrella term, the way mental-health professionals use the word *schizophrenia* as a catchall for any particular brand of crazy they can't identify. So when I say *hate*, I don't necessarily mean *hate*. I could also mean loathe, detest, abhor, dislike, despise or resent. See, isn't that kinder and gentler? If you think this makes you a better person than I am, good. You're the idiot that actually paid for this book.

For those of you thinking, *Geez, Joan seems a little angry*, you're half right. I am angry. I'm also fed up. I'm fed up with the morons and losers and cretins who are cluttering up the planet. Emma Lazarus wrote, "Give me your tired, your poor, your huddled masses yearning to breathe free." I didn't know she meant on my block. But being fed up and angry is better than being depressed. Psychologists tell us that depression is just anger turned inward, but I say, why waste your time? It is what it is and quite frankly I'd rather be angry than depressed. Why? Because antidepressants like Prozac, Wellbutrin and Zoloft can cause bloating—and I hate bloating!!! (I need to go back and add *bloating* to the list of things I hate. Is there anything worse than not being able to fit into a size two Valentino? I think not. Talk about depressing.)

I'm tired of people saying to me, "Joan, could you please try to be nice to Harry? He's depressed." No! Why should I have to work like a pack animal trying to be nice to Harry because that asshole's having a bad day?

Depression is a buzz kill for everyone involved except, of course, for the person who is actually depressed. That moody sourpuss gets all the attention, which only feeds their narcissism. I believe the great ~~Russian Italian Greek Polish~~ . . . philosopher Descartes said it best when he said, "I whine, therefore, I am." (Ah, he was Jewish.) But who really cares what Descartes said? You know where Descartes is today? Dead. So much for honesty being the best policy.

Before I move on, can I just say, I hate the French. (Note to self: Please put this on the list.) Why? Because those morons *still* think Jerry Lewis is fabulous, that's why.

For the few of you who are still reading this, I'll tell you what else I hate. I hate it when people say, "Let's invite Jane to the party. She's going through a difficult time." I say, "Fuck Jane. I'm paying top dollar for a caterer. Let Jane slash her wrists in *her* house." Introverted, depressed people suck the life out of a good party; angry, hateful people liven things up. You give me one person who is still angry the Third Reich was toppled, and I'll give you a great dinner party.

Did you ever walk into an amazing party, and you're strolling around, going from room to room, making small talk and slipping the nice serving spoons into your purse, when all of a sudden you run into a sweaty, angry guy in the library who looks like the Unabomber with better fashion sense? You know, the kind of guy who tells you that he doesn't care if the glass is half full or half empty, he only hopes it's broken and that Kenny G drinks from it and cuts his lips off and ruins his career. *That's* a good guest and he'll make it a great party.

Being with haters is much more entertaining than being with depressives, because haters are always, *always* willing to make a scene, God love them. And they'll make it anytime and anywhere: church, synagogue, Walmart—doesn't matter; they don't give a shit. *Those* are my kind of people.

Maybe this attitude can be attributed to my childhood. When I was a kid, making a scene was the worst, most egregiously horrible thing I could do. My parents hated that. If I had clubbed my grandmother to death like a baby seal with her walker, all my mother would have said was, "Joan! The neighbors can hear. Stop it. Don't make a scene!"

Watching a guest make a scene at a party is more fun than watching a blind man at a mime show. Everything at the party is going swimmingly—the piano player is noodling a Gershwin medley, martini glasses are clinking, people are chatting and then—*BOOM!*—from out of nowhere, for no apparent reason, and in less time than it takes Aretha Franklin to knock off a cheesecake, the guest goes from "Hello, hello," to shouting across the room at the hostess, "You're nothing more than a murdering, moneygrubbing whore, Mother!" I dare you to tell me that's not worth the price of a lovely, handwritten thank-you note?

As the title clearly states, I hate everyone and, like any self-respecting hater, I hate myself the most. All great haters do. I've been told that to this day, Charles Manson can't pass a mirror without going, "Bleghh." I know just how he feels.

And let me tell you why. It all goes back to my childhood. I was not a pretty girl. You know how some people comment on a person's appearance by saying things like, "She looks like her father"? Well, I actually *looked* like my father: mustache, man boobs, big thighs, hunched shoulders, sideburns. . . . All I needed was an enlarged prostate and you wouldn't have been able to tell us apart.

Right from the get-go, my parents didn't like me. When I was born, my mother asked, "Will she live?" The doctor said, "Only if you take your foot off her throat." I was the only baby in the maternity ward who had to take a bus home. My earliest childhood memory was watching my parents loosen the wheels on my stroller. For school lunch they'd make me peanut butter and strychnine sandwiches. Instead of a library card I had to carry a DNR warning. In seventh grade, I had a bad hair day and my mother went to court to fight for my right to die. My parents used to give me advice like "Take candy from strangers" and "Ask the guy in the raincoat if he owns a van."

When I was a *tween*—which is just a teen who hasn't given a blow job yet—I was fat. Fat, fat, fat. In spite of dieting, gagging, purging and drinking ipecac for lunch, I was a chubby girl. But rather than get angry or depressed I lived in a constant state of denial. I thought that being the only girl on the sumo team simply meant I was ahead of my time. In the hallway in our house my parents had this huge mirror and every time I walked by I thought, *Where'd those fuckers get the money to buy a Rubens? And they won't get me a new Barbie? Selfish pricks . . .*

Fat wasn't a condition, it was a way of life. In Girl Scouts, they had to let out my tent. *I* made Amos famous. I considered M&M's one of the food groups. On my first day of summer camp I said, "Where should I put my trunk?" The counselor said, "Wrap it around your tusks." A rapist grabbed me, took a look and said, "Maybe we could just be friends." My boyfriend needed a Sherpa to climb on top of me. I was the only person who ran with the bulls carrying a bottle of A.1. Steak Sauce. My husband used to *dress* me with his eyes. I sat shiva when my neighborhood Arby's closed.

And you wonder why I'm bitter?

Things are no better now that I'm in my decrepitude. Everything is falling apart . . . except for my face, which I've had lifted so many times I wear my earrings on my kneecaps. But my body has had it. I have chicken skin. I get "Wish You Were Here" cards from Perdue. Everything is sagging, and *I hate me!* My boobs are so low I had to put curb feelers on my nipples.

Getting old sucks! Everything is confusing. Sometimes late at night I wake up with this hot, moist feeling and I'm not sure if I'm having an orgasm or a stroke.

Look, I could go on and on and on telling you why I hate myself, but it's so self-centered . . . and I'm not like that. I'm a giver. So I'd rather branch out and start giving it to everyone else.

Forget the list at the top of the chapter. You want to know who and what I really hate!?! Then keep going . . .

FOR THE CHILDREN

The one thing I want to leave my children is an honorable name.

—TEDDY ROOSEVELT

Children make your life important.

—ERMA BOMBECK

Get in the car, you're going swimming.

—SUSAN SMITH

■

I hate children. Okay, it's not actually the *children* so much as it is the people who surround them. For example . . .

I hate people who think I'm interested in their children. I am *not* interested in their children. I'm barely interested in Melissa and What's-his-name, even though they say she's my child and he's my grandson.

Last week I was sitting on a plane and the guy next to me pulls out his wallet and says, "Wanna see pictures of my children?" What I wanted to say was, "Of course I do. When I woke up this morning I said to myself, 'Joan, what would make your day? . . . Hitting the lottery? . . . Winning an Oscar? . . . The unexpected death of any slightly younger comedian? No! Sitting on a cross-country flight looking at photos of some fat tire salesman's children? Why, yes, *that* would make my day. In fact, it would make my life worth living!'"

But I smiled and said to him, "Sure! I'd love to see pictures of your children! And you know what? I'd like to show *you* pictures of my colonoscopy. You have kids and I have polyps—let's swap!" Sometimes I'm too fucking nice.

I can't stand women who think that giving birth is some unique achievement that no one else has ever accomplished; that if it were not for their dropping Billy and Jimmy and Susie out of their wombs, the entire world would be an empty, desolate place—like a library in Alabama or a dentist's office in England.

Giving birth is not a new phenomenon; it's been happening since the beginning of time. Female dinosaurs were giving birth to baby dinosaurs long before female humans began giving birth to children. Except maybe in Wasilla, Alaska, where apparently they roamed the earth at the same time.

I hate people who make videos of their children's births. I'm aware of the fact that reality TV has blurred the lines between public and private behaviors, but there are some things that people really should keep private. For example, Woody Allen shouldn't order Chinese at a PTA luncheon. And nobody should have the cameras rolling when delivering a baby. But if you absolutely have to show people your childbirth movie, then at least have the decency to run the film backward and make the kid and all the gunk it comes out with disappear.

I've seen this sort of footage and it's not pretty. There are people crying and blood and guts all over the place. It's not a happy occasion, it's a crime scene; they ought to put yellow tape around the delivery room. This is not a home video; it's a new series on CBS: *CSI: Vulva.*

Unless you're giving birth to the Christ child or a Minotaur, I can wait until the kid's cleaned up to say hello. If I hear, "Do you want to see the head and shoulders?" you'd better be talking about shampoo.

I hate ugly children. When I see an ugly baby I feel enormous pressure to lie and be nice to the parents. I'll look at little Quasimodo in the bassinet and say things like, "His face has such character" or "He's going to be quite the lady-killer someday" or "She already has such personality." But if the kid is really, really, really ugly, I'll think *What the hell?* and just give up and say, "Where'd you buy the crib?"

And since we're all adults here, let's be brutally honest—most babies are not *actually* attractive. In fact, they're weird and freakish looking. A large percentage of them are squinty-eyed and bald and their faces are all mushed together, kind of like Renée Zellweger pushed up against a glass window.

I live next door to a single mother and she's got the ugliest baby in the entire world. This kid could frighten Wes Craven. This baby is so hairy it looks like Sasquatch in a bib. Thank God for small things—at least the hair on his head matches his tail. No one knows who the father is, but I think she must've screwed everyone in the Village of the Damned. When the kid was born and she brought him home (probably from the zoo) I didn't know what to say. All I came up with was, "At least he's not a twin."

Ugly adults should not be allowed to breed. Genetics is nothing new. If you're homely and your partner is homely, on a scale of one to Golda Meir, chances are the baby will be homely, too. When was the last time you saw homely parents with drop-dead gorgeous children? If I want to stare at someone with mismatched features I'll buy a Picasso.

I hate the women who run "the stroller patrol." Last week I was walking down Fifty-seventh Street, shopping for knockoffs and making snap judgments about the people walking by, when marching toward me was a tidal wave of women pushing strollers. They were marching eight across, like a German panzer division or Saddam Hussein's Red Army, barreling down the sidewalk, forcing everyone else to walk in the street. I said to one of them, politely, "Hey, you're taking up the entire sidewalk, bitch!" She scowled and yelled, "I have children!" I yelled back at her, "Well, next time give your husband a blow job and you won't! Why should I have to walk into oncoming traffic because you don't want to give a little head?"

I hate people who exploit missing children.

Nothing ruins a lovely evening like a cheesy news anchor rattling on about some poor kid who's wandered off or gone missing or been eaten by a dingo.

Every time I see one of those stories on HLN (which I think of as the Human Loss Network) about some new child that's gone missing I get so upset I have to grab the remote and change the channel. (Okay, *I* don't actually grab the remote. I have one of my assistants do it. I don't lift.)

It's bad enough a child is missing, but do I need to see some talking heads trying to leave *their* imprints on a terrible tragedy?

I saw one pretty little news anchor named Tiffany or Heather or Poppy open a story by saying, "It's every parent's nightmare to have their children go missing." Really? How the fuck would you know; you're twelve! What I really wanted to say to the little bitch was, "In hindsight, I'll bet Lyle and Erik Menendez's parents wouldn't have felt that way."

As you can tell, I'm the kind of person who's always looking for a silver lining and because of that I wonder if children gone missing is part of a larger plan; without them we never would have heard of the fabulous

Nancy Grace. Would Big N be a TV star, a household name and the symbol of abducted toddlers everywhere, or would she be making six dollars an hour as a cashier in a Piggly Wiggly or as a hostess in a roadside Stuckey's?

I love the end of the *Nancy Grace* show when Nancy puts up an on-screen profile of a real missing child. It's such a genuinely good thing to try and help find those missing kids, or at least help their families find some closure. But I hate it when the "missing child" she's profiling is thirty-five. It's one thing to profile little Amber, who was three years old when last seen at a campground near a lake; it's another to be profiling Mrs. Annette Roberts, who was forty-one and last seen driving away from her divorce lawyer's office in a red Camaro with her boyfriend, Vinnie.

I hate people who have thousands of children.

They say a child is the greatest gift a woman can receive. I don't know who "they" are, but "they" have clearly never been to Bergdorf's.

There is no reason for any family to have more than one or two children (unless you're the Osmonds or the Jacksons, and the little shits can support you from the get-go). If you have more than a couple of kids, you're not parents—you're hoarders. And hoarding is a disorder, not a gift.

Two kids? Fine. Built-in babysitter; one can keep an eye on the other so Mommy and Daddy can get liquored up in the den. Three? Okay, but only if the little one is subservient and willing to do scut work around the house like a long-suffering Polynesian slave. But four kids? Only if the eldest one is in a position to post bail, in case the parents snap because the other three drove them crazy.

Everyone thinks Angelina Jolie was the first celebrity baby hoarder, but she wasn't. Before Angelina there was Mia Farrow. Mia had an entire farm full of children. I think she got them at Costco. "I'll take two white ones, three brown ones, and a couple of those cute little yellow things."

When they ran out of regular kids she started adopting the wildly disfigured: "Give me the black torso, the Chinese girl with five legs, and how about that giant head sitting on the shelf?"

I hate the Octomom. Her uterus is like a sausage maker, churning out one pink link after another. She has fourteen children—*fourteen!!!* That's almost twice the number of people who watched *Kate Plus Eight*. Her vagina must be like the flume—the log ride at Six Flags. The hatch opens up and groups of screaming, wet children come flying out.

Octomom must have downtown lips like garage doors. Her gynecologist's office probably has a foreman. He says, "Spread 'em," and it looks like a dragon during the Chinese New Year's parade. This woman has had more crowned heads at her crotch than the entire royal family put together.

I had the one kid and it was enough for me. If there

is ever another head at my crotch, it'll be going in, not coming out.

I hate it when women breast-feed their children in public. I was on the crosstown bus and sitting across from me was a woman who was breast-feeding. There was the woman, there was her breast, and there was a face attached to it. The face belonged to a forty-one-year-old dermatologist named Lenny, which is strange, but whatever. I said to her, "Do you really need to do that in public?" And she snapped back, "Breast-feeding is a natural body function." I said, "So is urinating, but do you want me to take a piss right here on the bus?"

I love gay and lesbian parents. But I think we need a law that says lesbians and gay men have to raise their children *together*. This way, the kids would not only know how to build bookshelves, but they'd also instinctively know how to decorate them.

And for the record can I say that *just once* I would like to see a Chinese couple adopt a gay baby?

I hate child labor laws. For my clothing and jewelry lines I only hire underage, ugly, foreign children. I sneak them over from China, Singapore, and that country where instead of speaking they make those knock-knock sounds with their tongues. I put all the kids in giant barrels and ship them in the hull of a boat. And let me tell you something, they're happy to make the trip. Yes, the barrels are snug. So is the twelve-story walk-up they'll be sharing in New York, so let them get used to it. And the gentle rocking of that boat gives them a feeling of safety like they're back in their mother's womb, so they almost forget they're hungry.

I don't know why politicians complain about illegal immigrants. I love them! You can beat them like junk-yard dogs and they get up and go right back to the sewing machines! They work hard, they work cheap, and since they don't speak English, they don't complain when we "borrow" one of their kids. To me, it's a win-win!

I can't watch any more of those Christian Children's Fund TV commercials. You know, the ones with the kids who are covered with flies begging for food . . . What's the point in sending money? What restaurant is going to seat them? They're crawling with bugs. What's the correct wine with larvae? Flies are *not* accessories. And why are those children always named Mogowawa? Whatever happened to nice American names like Apple or Dweezil or Moon Unit?

I hate children who fall down wells, like Baby Jessica. Remember her? In 1987, at eighteen months old, she fell down an eight-inch-wide well in Midland, Texas, and became an overnight sensation. News crews from all over the world gathered for fifty-eight hours as policemen, firemen and rescue workers labored to pull this clumsy oaf out of a ditch. I know she was a toddler, but still, you've got to be some kind of klutz to drop through an opening that's only eight inches wide. She didn't fall down a well, she fell down Julia Roberts's mouth.

I hate baby talk. It's a complete waste of time and counterproductive to a child's development. Babies are born with no vocabulary. They're like dogs—or Snooki and JWoww—they respond to volume and tone and intonation. When you get a puppy you teach him the commands he'll need for the rest of his life, things like "sit" and "stay" and "roll over." You don't start talking to a puppy by saying "ruff, ruff, ruff." You would be wasting your time, making an ass out of yourself, *and* confusing the dog. I never spoke baby talk to Melissa. Right off the bat, the day she was born, I immediately began teaching her the commands she'd need for the rest of her life, things like, "Charge it" and "Prenup" and "No way, mister, not unless I get dinner first."

I hate dumb children. They slow down everyone else. How many times can you say, "No, Billy, that's not a bicycle, it's a pie"?

And there *are* dumb children. I'm not talking about slow children. I'm talking about children who are just plain, flat-out stupid. You know the type—the kid's in his fifth year of seventh grade. He's got a beard, he's got a mustache and he's got a son. He just can't get fractions.

I hate fraternal twins, especially those who don't even marginally look anything alike. You know what I mean—one twin is a tall, willowy blond girl with blue eyes and a killer smile, and the other is a hunched over Filipino boy with bad hair and a lazy eye. To me that's a scam; they're not twins, they're just two lonely people with a desperate need for attention.

I am fascinated by identical twins. Not in a weird yet creative, daring Dr. Mengele kind of way. More in a casual, "Oh, look how they're dressed alike even though they're fifty" kind of way. Twins who can't let go of their oneness have always creeped me out. Just because you shared a zygote doesn't mean you have to share a wardrobe. My dogs come from the same litter but I don't dress them in matching collars.

But I love Siamese twins (although I think the politically correct term is *conjoined twins*). It's so nice to see siblings bond. I have one sister and I won't even share my house with her, let alone my spleen.

Sometimes one of the conjoined twins gets married but the other one doesn't. How does that work, especially during sex? Does the married one say to the other one, "Don't look, Miltie and I are *schtupping*"? And what about when the twins are connected near the neck and one of the twins dies but the other doesn't, so the living one just has this head hanging off of her shoulder? It looks like an overblown epaulet. What does she say to people, "Oh, that's just Debbie. She's a good listener"?

I've always hated child stars, starting from way back when, when I was a child. The first child star I saw was Shirley Temple. She was six years old, two foot six and the biggest star in Hollywood. She wore ribbons in her hair, and frilly little pinafores and shiny patent-leather tap shoes—just like the boys in *Glee* do. I remember watching Shirley twirl around, spinning and tapping and singing "On the Good Ship Lollipop." And I remember vomiting as soon as she finished the song. I was so jealous; she had her own black man to dance with.

When Shirley was nine, she starred in *Heidi*, where she played a perky child who roamed the Swiss Alps with a weird old man and some sheep. She also starred in *Little Miss Marker*, where she played a perky child who roamed horse racing tracks with a creepy old bookmaker. And who could forget Shirley in *Wee Willie Winkie,* where she played a perky child who roams around India with a creepy, militant prisoner? Do we see a pattern, *mes amies?* This all seems very Jaycee Dugard, to me.

But the main reason I hate Shirley Temple is *Rebecca of Sunnybrook Farm.* At the same time she was starring in *Rebecca, I* was in development of the Jewish version of the exact same story, *Miriam of East Flatbush.* The bitch stole my idea.

To this day I hate Margaret O'Brien. We're about the same age, if she's still alive. As a child she was a star on screen; I was on antibiotics for measles and mumps and the STD I got from the cantor. I remember going to the movies when I was seven and watching her up on the screen in *Journey for Margaret* and thinking, *I can play a war orphan, too, you shanty Irish whore!* I've followed her career for my entire life and let me tell you, nothing, not even the birth of my daughter or the death of Helen Reddy's career made me quite as happy as when Margaret O'Brien got fat.

I always loathed Mickey Rooney. Not personally—I don't know him. I'm sure he's a lovely man, even if he does sometimes forget to wear his partial bridge when going out in public. But the young Mickey Rooney was very unsettling. For starters, he went from being a child star to an adult star without growing an inch or gaining a pound. He stayed the same exact size his entire life. I hate that. Think of the money he's saved on sweaters alone.

I've always been frustrated by the dwarf-midget continuum. (And FYI, I refuse to say "little person." I hate euphemisms. I know the difference between midgets and dwarves, but I don't know the difference between midgets, dwarves and people who are just tiny, which drives me crazy because I don't know whether to put on my "oh, isn't she cute" face or my "your parents shouldn't be allowed to breed" face.

It's not easy making conversation with tiny people. For starters, I hate bending. I believe in making eye contact, but in order to do that with a tiny person I have to hunch over like Renfield walking through

Dracula's cave. I think developing scoliosis is a big price to pay for conversation with someone who's little. Plus, I'm usually in heels. It's a risk. Do I risk breaking a pair of expensive Manolo Blahniks just to talk to Tiny Timmy? I think not.

The other complication in talking to someone who's tiny is that you know that they know that you know they're tiny and that you're pretending not to notice. Can you say *awkward*? How about *exhausting*?

Which brings me back to Mickey Rooney, who, in his dotage, is not half the man he used to be. (Feel free to write you own joke here.)

Mickey made huge hit movies like *Boys Town* and *The Adventures of Huckleberry Finn*, but he's most famous for the two hundred fifty thousand Andy Hardy movies he made, playing opposite Judy Garland—classics like *Andy Hardy's Double Life* (which today would be *Andy Hardy on the DL*), *Andy Hardy's Blonde Trouble*, and my favorite, *Andy Hardy Develops a Cold Sore*.

The fact that Mickey Rooney spent years trying to convince audiences that Judy Garland would actually fall in love with a straight man was not only ridiculous, but, quite frankly (to a fag-hag like me), wildly offensive.

One of Mickey's other big hit movies was *National Velvet*, where he starred opposite a horse . . . and a stallion named Pie. I know what you're thinking: *Elizabeth Taylor wasn't fat back then*. You're right, she wasn't, but there *were* signs of things to come. Watch the movie again, closely this time—you'll see a beautiful, young

Elizabeth Taylor . . . licking her lips when a wagon full of hay passes by or smiling and furrowing her unibrow when the blacksmith comes through town with new shoes.

Okay, to be honest, I didn't hate Elizabeth Taylor, I was just jealous of her. She had those striking, unbelievable violet eyes and all I got were purple spider veins. It just wasn't fair.

It's not just the old-time Hollywood child stars I abhor; modern-day child stars can suck, too. Macaulay Culkin? Tell me he doesn't need a near-death experience to whip him into shape? Oh, wait—he's already had one. Remember the fire? Macaulay's not much more than thirty and already he's been married, divorced, had a house fire and made three comebacks. I have one word for this: *neeeeeedy.*

I hate Miley Cyrus and Britney Spears and Lindsay Lohan and all those other Hollywood trampettes. I don't hate them because they're rich and famous but because they became stars in a time of rehab. Judy Garland got all fucked up on drugs and alcohol and wound up living in Central Park; Lindsay Lohan gets all fucked up on drugs and alcohol and winds up living on Dr. Drew's couch. It's just not fair.

The cast of *Glee* turns my stomach. Not because they're child stars, but because they're grown-up adults *playing* child stars. You know that cute Asian boy who plays a freshman? In real life he's a thirty-year-old man and he's upside down on a mortgage in Burbank. The only way Lea Michele is in high school is if she's part of some bizarre religious cult and she's come back to school with bombs strapped to her boobs and she's planning to blow the place to kingdom come. The only true character on *Glee* is the fat girl because in real life she is a fat girl. (But there is a bright side to being fat. When people talk about you in later life, they will never say, "Gee, she looks haggard and old." You'll always look the same to them so you'll always hear what you've always heard: "Same old pig. Her *tuchas* is still the size of Arizona." See, another silver-lining moment.)

The other thing that bothers me about *Glee* is that everyone in that high school is happy, even the homos. On *Glee* all the homo kids are smiling and giggly and they spend every day singing in the halls. When I went to high school the homos spent most of their days hiding in their lockers crying. If I came home from school and sang to my mother she would have slapped me in the face and said, "Stop singing! You're Jewish! Everyone hates us."

No one in my high school was happy. If we had our own TV show it would have been called *Gloom*. In my high school yearbook Sylvia Plath was the one voted "Miss Congeniality." The only ones in my school who weren't completely miserable were the cheerleaders—and that's only because they were so busy taking home-pregnancy tests they didn't have time to get depressed.

Can I just mention that I hated *Dennis the Menace* **and** *Leave It to Beaver?* What's with the mawkish rhyming? The kid was a bratty little boy so they called him Dennis the Menace? If he was a gay Jew would they have called him Schlomo the Homo? And FYI, I always thought *Leave It to Beaver* should have been about Katharine Hepburn's sex life.

The only child stars I like are the ones who are troubled because when they grow up they become troubled adults. And without troubled adults Dr. Phil would be doing pro bono work in New Jersey.

Healthy child stars become healthy adults: Ron Howard, Brooke Shields, Jodie Foster . . . *Boooooooring!!!*

I love that Danny Bonaduce (from *The Partridge Family*) was a junkie, or that Maureen McCormick, who played Marcia Brady, was fucking the entire bunch, including Alice the maid. Britney passed out with a baby on the dashboard and a Bud Lite in her crotch? Fan-tastic! Or Winona Ryder getting caught stuffing panty hose down her bra? Bingo!! I'm particularly fond of Mackenzie Phillips; apparently while she was on *One Day at a Time* she was not only an alcoholic and a dope fiend, but she was also having sex with her father! Talk about a Lifetme movie of the week . . . I mean, I loved the Mamas and the Papas, but not like that.

But my two favorite child stars are the Olsen twins; those two girls have not a shred of talent or a brain cell between them and yet they've become billionaires. I love them, I respect them, I envy them. I especially like the one with the eating disorder. That girl's a perfect date—you don't have to spend much on dinner and you don't have to buy her really expensive fashions because when it comes to clothing all she's really concerned with is absorbency. Plus, she's worth a billion dollars *and* she's single!!! You know, now that gay marriage is becoming legal maybe I should encourage Melissa to consider lesbianism.

And the thing I hate most about child stars are the people around them: agents, managers, publicists, I hate them, too. (More on that in the showbiz chapter.)

NOTABLE TV MOTHER/DAUGHTER TEAMS

Mrs. Brady and her bunch. Carol had a great relationship with Cindy and Jan and Marcia. Why wouldn't she? Alice the maid had to do all the heavy lifting and deal with the girls' crying and whining and cramping while all Carol had to do was keep her hair in that stupid '70s shag cut, make the occasional pitcher of lemonade, and try to look interested while Mike Brady spewed out his long-winded, common-sense homilies about family life, while sitting in the closet.

Shirley Partridge and her family. We all thought Shirley was the best mother and had a perfect relationship with Laurie. In reality, to this day Laurie is somebody with a bad twitch you shouldn't make any sudden moves around. Mother of the Year Shirley Partridge not only forced the entire family to go out on the road and sing (sort of like white Jacksons), she made them all live in an old school bus so they could pick up extra cash smuggling undocumented Salvadoran immigrants north to pick oranges.

Samantha and Tabitha Stephens. Sam assumed her daughter, Tabitha, was a witch because she twitched her nose. Ever heard of drugs, Samantha? That wasn't pixie dust Tabitha was buying from Dr. Bombay a gram at a time. Both the Stephens women were so strung out, half the time they didn't even notice when two different actors played the role of Darrin.

Carrie Bradshaw and Samantha Jones. Okay, technically they weren't mother and daughter but given the age difference they could have been. (They obviously weren't cycle sisters, either, because by the time they met Samantha had already gone through menopause.) Yet despite the vast, yawning, gaping age difference between them, they developed such a deep friendship they became almost like Oprah and Gayle. If Carrie and Samantha had become lesbian lovers the name of the show would have to be changed to *Very Occasional Sex After the First Six Months and the City*.

Sharon and Kelly Osbourne. I love the way they put aside their differences and united for a common purpose: trying to figure out what the hell Ozzy was saying.

Lucy and Lucie. Or as I like to think of them, Ball and Chain. Poor little Lucie, she only had one walk-on part in her parents' sitcom. I think Lucy's got some 'splainin' to do about that. Also, Lucy named little Lucie with an *ie* instead of a *y* to make sure that the Lucy everybody loved was *her*. Everyone did love Lucy, especially Lucy.

Mrs. Cunningham and Joanie. Not what I'd call a textbook example of motherhood, even for the 1950s. Instead of keeping Joanie away from bad boys who wore leather and rode motorcycles, Mrs. Cunningham allowed them to live in a room above the garage. Girls like Joanie usually get in trouble. If the Fonz told Joanie to "sit on it," she probably would have. Mrs. C was lucky that Joanie only loved Chachi. Joanie could have loved coochie.

Angela and Mona. Angela was constantly embarrassed by her mother's sex life. The question in that family wasn't "who's the boss?" but "who's on top?"

Marge and Lisa Simpson. I *looooove* Marge Simpson. She taught Lisa to lie about her age because after twenty years on the air, Marge is still only thirty-four.

Roseanne and Darlene. I could relate to their hardscrabble, blue-collar existence because once Melissa and I almost had to fly coach. Thank God there was a death in first class, which freed up a nice aisle seat for me, while Melissa fit beautifully in the overhead compartment.

Kris Jenner and Kim Kardashian. Most mothers would be horrified if one of their daughters made a sex tape. Not Kris. She used the sex tape as a screen credit to get Kim into the Screen Actors Guild. Who says "love" isn't a four-letter word?

Mama Walton and her daughter (pick one). The Waltons spent so much time saying "good night," it's a wonder Ma and Pa had the strength to make more little Waltons. The show could have been more interesting if they'd given John Boy a gender identity crisis like Chaz Bono. I would have liked to tune in one night and hear, "Good night, John Girl!" The show became much more interesting after Grandma Walton had the stroke and couldn't speak, because then you couldn't tell if she was grimacing in pain, smirking in

33

disgust, or nodding approvingly. Viewing fun for the whole family!

Melissa and Me. *See all of the above.*

TICK-TOCK

There are four types of old people:

- ◆ Regular
- ◆ Old and annoying
- ◆ Old and infirm
- ◆ Just not dead yet

■

Why do I hate old people? Because they smell, that's why. It's a fact. Check out the *New York Times* Science section. Right there, between "nuclear waste" and "raw sewage," it says, and I quote, "a team of renowned international scientists and olfactory experts have proven beyond a shadow of a doubt that old people—particularly those from the mothball generation—smell. And Mrs. Estelle Neiburg in apartment #2F is especially fetid."

Why do old people buy in bulk? Whenever I'm in a hurry, directly in front of me at the supermarket there's a one-hundred-eighty-five-year-old person standing with ninety-three jars of mayonnaise. Talk about an optimist! He's not going to make it through the check-out counter. Unless God likes chicken salad sandwiches, the guy's an idiot. The only thing old people could use in large amounts is formaldehyde.

I don't want to hear about "the good old days." I have no idea who Clara Bow—*Beau?*—was and I don't care unless I was mentioned in her will. But I do know that things *weren't* better before air-conditioning, limousines, vibrators and stool softeners.

I hate old people who make irritating noises with their lips. You're sitting there in the sunroom with Grandpa watching *Wheel of Fortune,* when he sighs and blurts out, "That Vanna White sure knows her alphabet," and then for no apparent reason starts making smacking sounds with his lips and gums. He's not eating or drinking anything. He's not even drooling yet (that doesn't usually happen until eleven o'clock), and he's not having a seizure. Just twenty minutes of slurping like a dog licking his crotch. Look, I read somewhere—probably in the same *New York Times* article—that you're not supposed to hit old people, but sometimes a good whack on the nose with a newspaper is all they understand.

I hate early-bird specials. Who the hell eats dinner at two o'clock? I know seniors are on fixed incomes, but to save eighty-six cents by eating dinner before lunch is insane. And people talk. I know; I'm one of those people. When I see the Weinsteins hobbling into IHOP at 1:45 for dinner I'm not thinking, "How smart. What good planners. A penny saved . . ." I'm thinking,

"Cheap humps. You're the reason we Jews are chased and hunted down all over the world."

On top of that, they only order half a chicken, take two bites, then put it in a doggie bag to take home, where it lasts them for six months. Anne Frank didn't hoard food like this, and that bitch was hungry.

I hate old people who actually tell you how they are when you ask them. So never say, "How are you?" to an old person. This just opens a door you do not want to go through. And "How are you feeling, Mr. Lubell?" is even worse. The old coot starts whining, "Thank you for asking me how I am, Joan—it *is* you, Joan? I have glaucoma now. I used to have cataracts but things have gotten worse. I can't drive anymore so I don't go out much. I had to eat cat food last night and I'm allergic to Friskies, so I got this rash all over my stomach. I scratched so much I started bleeding. Which is bad because I'm anemic, my doctor says. Not that I have a real doctor. He's a quack from the clinic. I have to go there, as I have no money ever since my son-in-law stole everything from the bank. I'd ask you to sit down but I have no extra room on my scooter, which they're repossessing on Friday for late payments. And then I'll have to have a neighbor drag me to the store so I can buy day-old bread and fish soup, which I'm probably allergic to, as shellfish makes me break out in these boils, and when I go by all the kids will think, 'There goes poor Mr. Lubell. He's disgusting and Mom says he's a perv and and and . . .'" And all *I'm* thinking is, "I hope you're not allergic to mahogany or pine because I'm going to kill you right now."

I hate old people who say, "I'm eighty-nine years young!" It's not cute. It's stupid and irritating. You're not eighty-nine years "young." You're six years beyond "good-bye."

I hate it when old people are referred to as "feisty." "Feisty" means Nana got all defensive and angry when you had the nerve to point out that she accidentally shit all over your new car seats. And not only did she not even apologize for the blood in the stool that left permanent stains on your beautiful beige Corinthian leather, but she got even "feistier" when you mentioned the smell that the little pine tree on the dashboard cannot disguise.

I hate the elderly who refuse to die. Old people are like dairy products—they have an expiration date, and if they're left on the shelf too long they go sour. Every time I pass some *altacocker* sitting at a card table, hunched over and wheezing, I want to yell, "Get in the box, Mildred! It's time to get in the box!"

I hate old bodies. Which is why I've had mine renovated six hundred times. I've undergone more reconstruction than Baghdad. My plastic surgeon is on staff at Restoration Hardware. I keep a crane in the bedroom to make sure my ass doesn't hit the floor. Everything drops when you get old . . . boobs, bellies, butts, everything. Last week my friend Miriam was sagging so much she broke a hip when she tripped over her vagina.[*]

I hate old men who have no hair left on their legs and their calves look like pieces of wax fruit. Smooth legs on a man is creepy. When I'm playing footsie late at night I shouldn't be the one in the bed with the stubble.

I hate old men who have hair in their ears. A widower whose eustachian tubes look like a rain forest is not a turn-on. Instead of Q-tips he needs a super mop. I knew one guy who had such a jungle in his ears I expected Dian Fossey to come waltzing out with a couple of her prized gorillas, Tojo and Millie.

I hate old men who wear their pants hiked up to their nipples. It pulls their balls up so high it looks like they're smuggling children in their diapers.

I hate old people and phlegm. Old people are obsessed with phlegm. All day long they're gagging and hacking and coughing. . . . They spend more time with yellow goop in their mouths than a hooker in Chinatown.

I hate old men who try to act jaunty and flirt. He says, "I like to pleasure my women."

---

[*]Talk about turning lemons into lemonade. She said she's glad her vagina dropped because every time there's an earthquake she's suctioned to the floor.

And I'm thinking, *Yeah? Then pick up the check.*

He says, "Here's my gal."

I think, *I'd rather be mauled by a Bengal tiger than let anyone think I'm "your gal."*

He says, "I'm with the two prettiest girls in the room!"

I think, *If you could see, you old moron, you'd know there are only two girls in the room to start with.*

I hate old people who won't make concessions to age.
If you can't see over the steering wheel or know there's a stroller pinned under your car's bumper you shouldn't be driving anymore.

"No, no, I can still drive!"

"Grandpa, there's a Buick in the kitchen. No, you can't."

I hate old people who dangle carrots:

"You know, you're in my will."

"That doesn't cut it, Granny. I've seen your apartment. You've got nothing I want. I've never liked Hummel."

I love going through my high school yearbook with a highlighter, x-ing out the ones who are dead.
I'm happy to report that as of this writing, pages twenty-eight through forty-six, inclusive, are gone.

Out of the blue my sister called and asked, "Did you hear that Jacob Schwartz, the guy who stood you up at the prom, died?"

I perked right up. "Natural causes?"

"No," she said. "Suspicious circumstances. Something about a daughter-in-law and a hypodermic needle filled with air."

I was so happy I could barely contain myself.

The only good thing about age is that sooner or later all of the SOBs who dumped you are going to die.

The words "old people" and "sex" should never be part of the same conversation. When I hear Granny use the word "multiple" it better be followed by "vitamin" not "orgasm." I just don't want to hear Nana talk about sex.

"You know, Joan, my butcher has a cock the size of Cairo." *Blech!*

I don't need the image of Granny giving head. The only things Granny's mouth should be used for are chewing and clearing the loose phlegm that keeps accumulating because her lungs are starting to fail.

How Do You Know You're Too Old for Sex?

1. **When there's always a wet spot.**
2. **When you give a blow job you can't get off your knees.**
3. **During sex he calls out his nurse's name.**
4. **When it takes a third party to get him off of you.**

I hate faking orgasm with an old man. You work and you work and then the whole thing's a total waste of time because you forget to moan in his good ear.

And finally, the only good thing about old sex is you never have to suffer the humiliation of a one-night stand, because there's no such thing. Just to get him out of the car, into the house, up the stairs, on the bed, on you, off of you, down the stairs, rediapered, and back into the car . . . minimum, four days. That's not a quickie, that's a relationship.

SIGNS THAT YOUR FAMILY HATES YOU NOW THAT YOU'RE OLD

- They take the batteries out of your "I've Fallen and I Can't Get Up" necklace.

- They turn your room into a crafts studio while you are still living in it.

- They find your hospice nurse on craigslist.

- At Thanksgiving they push you into the oven to check on the turkey.

- They replace your Astroglide with Krazy Glue.

- Your Secret Santa is Jack Kevorkian's disciple.

- They send you on an all-expense-paid meditation retreat on Three Mile Island.

DEATH BE NOT PROUD

Mahatma Gandhi once said, "I am prepared to die, but there is no cause for which I am prepared to kill."

Apparently Gandhi never tried to get a table at Spago.

■

Everyone dies—except maybe Betty White, and I think its high time someone pushed that bitch in front of a train because I'm sick and tired of losing the "sassy grandma" roles to her. Betty White is ninety million years old. Her first résumé is on a cave wall in France. She put the Sutra in Kama. She read *Beowulf* in installments. She's been on three hundred TV shows, won a boatload of Emmys and earned a trillion dollars. If I had just one of those things I'd be so happy—or at least a lot less bitter.

To be fair, it hasn't been all roses for Betty; she hasn't *shtupped* anybody since Allen Ludden died. The password is "dried out."

I love the obituaries. Every morning when I get up, the first thing I do is wax and read the paper. Well, not the first thing; the first thing I do is have my live-in plastic surgeon do a quick touch-up on my chin and neck and *then* I wax and read the paper. Okay, not the whole paper, just a couple of sections. I read the gossip section to see if any celebrity friends got caught up in a scandal that I can exploit and take advantage of, and then I read the obituaries because I want to start my day off right. To me, obituaries are just wedding announcements without the pictures. I read the obituaries carefully, the way Lindsay Lohan reads her Miranda rights.

The first thing I do is check out the Jews who died because Jewish funerals have the best catering, and if I just happen to be in the neighborhood when they're doing the service, I figure why not pop in for a nosh?

I hate it when the obituary doesn't tell you *how* the person died. They make you guess. It's early in the morning and my brain's not firing on all cylinders yet. Would it kill them to just say, "Murray Weintraub, fifty-eight, mumps"?

Sometimes you can tell what happened by reading the "in lieu of flowers" portion of the obit. For example, if it says, "In lieu of flowers, please send money to the Painful Rectal Itch Foundation." Now you not only know why he died but also why he couldn't sit still in church.

You can also tell a lot about a person and their family by reading their obituary. And not just reading what's printed, but reading into what's *not* printed, what they left out.

For example, if it says, "no immediate survivors" it means the deceased was gay and the family refuses to acknowledge his or her partner because they want all the money in the estate for themselves.

"Services will be private" means the deceased was a son of a bitch and had no friends, colleagues or passing acquaintances. Or he was a serial killer and had no friends, colleagues or passing acquaintances because he offed them.

I hate it when I read an obit that says, "Molly Fishman, 102, suddenly." Excuse me? She's 102! How sudden could it have been? She's been old since the Truman administration. The woman's been hunched over in her wheelchair, with her tongue on the footrest since 1992; shouldn't someone have seen her demise coming???

I hate people who die of natural causes; they just don't understand the moment. It's the grand finale, act three, the eleven o'clock number—make it count!

One of my friends called me and said, "My father-in-law died." I tried to pretend I cared so I said, "Are you okay?" He said, "He was ninety-eight, of course I'm okay. He didn't die bungee jumping, he just didn't get up."

When a seventy-three-year-old calls you and says, "My mother died," don't bother to say, "Of what." You know already that the answer won't be pole-vaulting or mixed martial arts.

If you're going to die, die interesting! Is there anything worse than a boring death? (Other than a Charlie Rose marathon on PBS?) I think not. When my time comes I'm going to go out in high style. I have no intention of being sick or lingering or dragging on and on and boring everyone I know. I have no intention of coughing and wheezing for months on end. One morning you'll wake up and read a headline: JOAN RIVERS FOUND DEAD . . . ON GEORGE CLOONEY'S FACE. CLOONEY WAS SO BEREFT ALL HE COULD SAY WAS, "XJFHFYRNEM."

I hate cancer. It's a big snore. *Booorrrringggg!* Everyone's got it these days. Lung cancer, bone cancer, brain cancer—it's all the same, and the treatment's always the same: chemo, radiation, whining and baldness (and not a good kind of baldness like Patrick Stewart or Ben Kingsley, but a "Gee, there's no way to accessorize that" kind of baldness).

I hate my friends who are breast cancer survivors. They're always whining, "I lost a breast, I lost a breast." You lost ten pounds. Shut up, bitch, you're down a size!

I find face cancer riveting. It's like leprosy without the flaking. One day you're smiling for all the world to see; the next day, you're looking under the couch for your nose.

The actress Nancy Kulp, who played Miss Hathaway on the *Beverly Hillbillies*, died from a nasty case of face cancer. Every day a little bit of Nancy fell away. Not that it was a huge loss; hers was not a pretty face. In fact, she was homely even by lesbian standards. But give her credit—she died interestingly. She'd lost half her face, her jaw, her tongue. She looked like Señor Wences's fist but she kept on talking, God bless her.

I hate hospice nurses who provide "palliative care." Palliative care means "keep the old coot medicated so she dies in her sleep and I don't have to smother her and then deal with the 'angel of death' inquiries that are sure to follow and mess up my non-refundable week in Cabo."

I love funerals! To me a funeral is just a red carpet show for dead people. It's a chance for mourners from all walks of life to accessorize basic black, and to make a fashion statement that is bold enough to draw attention away from the bereaved but subtle enough so that no one knows that it's happening. And, it's a great way to have quiet fun. For example, I love to write nasty things about the dead person in the condolence book and then sign their grandchildren's names.

I hate people who try to make you feel better. Like the neighbor who says, "Don't forget, the first part of 'funeral' is 'fun'!" Or the minister who says, "He's in a better place now." I'm tempted to yell out, "No he's not. He had a house in the Hamptons. What's wrong with you?"

I went to one funeral and the rabbi said very movingly, "Ashes to ashes, dust to dust," and then he ruined it by adding, "and Sylvia to Saks."

When I die (and yes, Melissa, that day will come; and yes, Melissa, everything's in your name), I want my funeral to be a huge showbiz affair with lights, cameras, action. . . . I want Craft services, I want paparazzi and I want publicists making a scene! I want it to be Hollywood all the way. I don't want some rabbi rambling on; I want Meryl Streep crying, in five different accents. I don't want a eulogy; I want Bobby Vinton to pick up my head and sing "Mr. Lonely." I want to look gorgeous, better dead than I do alive. I want to be buried in a Valentino gown and I want Harry Winston to make me a toe tag. And I want a wind machine so that even in the casket my hair is blowing just like Beyoncé's.

I love the death reel at the Oscars, where they honor all of the people in Hollywood who died during the past year. A good death reel can almost compensate for five hours of French actors trying to make adorable acceptance speeches. One of my favorite things to do is guess which one of the dead actors will get the most applause and who's going to be surprisingly underappreciated. It's tricky, you can't always tell. Some years the most applause goes to whoever died young and tragically; other years it goes to the old and beloved. I really love it when the Academy accidentally leaves a deadie out of the reel and the error of omission becomes a huge cause célèbre. Remember a few years ago when they left Bea

Arthur out of the death reel? Bea Arthur! How did they leave Bea Arthur out? She was in *Mame*; she was in *All in the Family*; she was in *Maude*; she was a Golden Girl, for God's sake! Bea was not only one of Hollywood's leading ladies, she was one of Hollywood's leading men. There are still people talking about that horrible gaffe and to this day, in Beverly Hills, when that subject comes up, people say Bea Arthur's name in a muffled whisper like people used to do when they said "cancer."

As I get older, I'm going to a lot more funerals, and let me tell you something, it's a great pick-up scene. A graveside funeral is like eHarmony for the bereaved. I went to my friend's husband's funeral a few weeks ago and some accountant from Queens kept hitting on her. He said things like, "So, you're single?" And, "You know, black really brings out your eyes." And, "I love the way you shovel . . . what are you doing after the kaddish?" My friend was horrified. Not so horrified she didn't give him a hummer in the back of his Lexus, but still . . .

At funerals I like to play a little game called Watch the Widow. I can tell just by her demeanor if she loved him, if he left her anything, or if she's happy that he's finally gone. If she sobs uncontrollably, she knows he was cheating on her and down the road she might be implicated in his death. If she seems completely distracted she's probably been having an affair, maybe with his brother or his doctor. And if she's distracted and breathing heavily, she's been having an affair with the undertaker and can't decide whether to weep quietly or get a quickie in the toilet.

I hate planning funerals. No one ever says "thank you." I've planned a couple of funerals and not one person has ever come up to me afterward and said, "Joan, what a lovely spread. I hope someone else dies just so we can come back for the lovely *babka* and white-fish salad you put out." And what about dressing the corpse, you think it's easy? It's a thankless job. You have to be conscious of both the mourners *and* the fashion. It's the last time you're going to see your friend Helen, so you'd better dress her right. I have one rule: Don't listen to what her kids say; she's not going down in pleats. No woman, not even Kate Moss, should be buried in pleats. They accentuate the hips.

I hate casket shopping. No matter what you buy, you're wrong. A simple pine box screams, "Cheapo." And one of those huge, brightly colored metal things looks like a float in a Puerto Rican Day parade. If you put a Jewish star or a cross on top of the coffin someone always mutters under their breath, "He wasn't that religious," but if you don't do it, you hear, "Jesus Christ, how much could it have been for a cross?"

I have a business idea: custom-designed caskets. This way nobody can whine or complain. Design a coffin that speaks specifically to the person who is going to be buried in it. Let's say for example, that while the deceased was alive he liked to surf. Why not design a coffin filled with sand and with openings at the end so that his toes can stick out and hang ten! Get it?

When Victoria Beckham goes, put her in a giant shopping bag.

I knew a woman who spent most of her life on prescription drugs. How cool would it have been to put her in a casket filled with cotton and a childproof lid?

I've always wanted to design a coffin for a stripper. Why should anyone have to worry about whether Bubbles should have an open or closed casket? I'd design one that has a little window that goes up when the mourner puts in a quarter. Who says you can't be sad and horny at the same time?

But when I die none of this is going to matter because I'm not really going anywhere. I'm not going to be buried because I don't like damp and cold.

I think cremation is the way to go for some people, and for different reasons. I had one friend who had her husband cremated and put him in her douche bag so she could run him through one more time.

I had another friend whose husband's will said that if she didn't visit every day she wouldn't get any money. So she had him cremated and sprinkled his ashes in Bergdorf Goodman, and hasn't missed a day in twelve years. (On 9/11, in the horror of the moment she was so upset she managed to get there twice. Now that's a widow!)

Then again, maybe when I go toes up I want to be stuffed and put on the living room couch, then when people come over Melissa can say, "Sit down and don't mind Mom. She's on vocal rest for her new play."

MY FAVORITE CELEBRITY DEATHS

Isadora Duncan

Isadora went for a ride in the car but couldn't decide if she should wear a scarf or a choker. Turns out she wore both.

Attila the Hun

For all the marauding, torture and trampling, the head Hun died from a nosebleed on his wedding night. Now that's what I call rough sex.

Jayne Mansfield

I begged her to buy a car with extra headroom, but did she listen? No.

Catherine the Great

Rumors abound. One rumor is that she had a stroke while going to the bathroom. If this is true then you know why fiber is important. The conventional and far more fun story is that she died while having sex with a horse. The horse was being lowered onto her when the pulleys broke and down came Secretariat, turning Catherine the Great into Catherine the Smushed. You want irony? The horse's favorite position was doggie style.

Honestly, I don't think Catherine's relationship with the horse would have worked, anyway. First of all, he didn't know how to hold her. Secondly, every night when they went back to the castle, all the horse wanted to do was watch *Seabiscuit* over and over and over. And finally, the horse wasn't Jewish.

Ramon Novarro

Two male prostitutes suffocated the Latin movie star to death with a lead dildo that was given to him forty-five years earlier by Rudolph Valentino. My question: Who keeps a dildo for forty-five years?

Joan of Arc

She kept complaining to hotel management that she was chilly because her room was drafty. Next time, she'll learn to keep her mouth shut. Served her right.

Natalie Wood

After she drowned off the coast of Catalina Island all we kept hearing was "Natalie Wood hated water;" "Natalie Wood couldn't swim." Then why was she on a boat in the middle of the fucking night? I'm deathly afraid of Kirstie Alley; you don't see me showing up at the Scientology Center at 2:00 A.M. with a box of Twinkies.

Marvin Gaye

Music superstar Marvin Gaye was shot to death by his father. In court the father said, "This is probably the worst thing I've ever done." *Probably??????*

Steve Irwin, the Crocodile Hunter

He was being his adventurous self when he was stung by a stingray and died. So I say to all of you: Forget crocodiles. Be a *bargain* hunter—no one was ever killed by a Louis Vuitton knockoff.

Butterfly McQueen

She survived the burning of Atlanta in *Gone With the* Wind, but died while cooking in her own apartment. Since that day I like to think of her as Batter Fried McQueen.

Sigmund Freud

Died of throat cancer in 1939. He blamed it on his mother.

LOVE SUCKS

I was married for twenty years and then my husband killed himself. After that for seven years I lived with a one-legged war hero. I left him when I found out he'd been hopping into the sack with another woman.

■

I hate "love at first sight." Unless you're Stevie Wonder there's no such thing. Stevie can walk up to a woman, feel her face and shriek, "Isn't she lovely." But for the rest of us, love is a process—like filing taxes or doing monthly colon cleansings.

Do you think Franklin Roosevelt took one look at Eleanor and thought, *Back that thing up here, bitch*? Do you think Siegfried saw Roy across a crowded room and said, "I'd like to put my tiger in his tent?"

My late husband, Edgar, and I got married after knowing each other for four days. He had no idea who I really was. Edgar had no clue that the hair he loved to touch he could take with him to the office. By the time I took off the hair, the contacts, the partial bridges and the padded bra, he didn't know whether to get into the bed or into the drawer.

I hate women who say, "I knew he was the one." How could you know that? Did you already fuck everyone else? Yet with Edgar it *was* love at first sight for me; he was simply everything I wanted in a man: breathing and not repulsed.

I hate dating. Women go on dates to get free meals. Men go on dates to get free feels. And lesbians go on dates to get camping equipment and unattractive footwear.

Even as a young girl I was terrible at dating. Compared to me, Carrie had more fun at her prom. Guys didn't try to get me into the backseat of a car; they tried to get me under the back wheels. I said to one guy, "Why don't you slip into something more comfortable?" He slipped into someone else's apartment.

I hate first dates. Why is it always dinner and a movie? Why not dinner and a trip to Europe, or dinner and a new car, or, if I'm in failing health, dinner and a new valve? Men think going to a movie is a safe first date: They don't have to make conversation and for eight bucks they might even be able to cop a feel. Or, if they're on a date with me, four bucks, as I'm a senior citizen. And two bucks if they feel me before 3:00.

I hate women who date much younger men. I'll never be a cougar. I don't like younger men. I don't ever want to wake up in the morning and wonder, *Is this my date or did I give birth last night?* Yet for some it works. I have one friend who dated a guy who was so much younger that when she bought him the book *The Joy of Sex* he sat down and colored in it.

I hate dating small talk. People don't tell the truth. Chatting about the weather or movies or books is a complete waste of time. I say be honest right from the get-go. If he says, "How are you?" tell him the truth: "Constipated. I haven't had a good shit since 9/11." Get to it right away: "I believe in bestiality, incest and sixth-trimester abortions. I'm in favor of shooting old people who complain about the room being too drafty, and I loathe people who find fault with dogfighting. I have halitosis, my lower jaw clicks when I chew and when I eat soft food it comes out of my nose." By the time you've finished the appetizers you'll know if the evening is going to end up in a warm bed or a shallow grave.

I hate couples that make out in public. I always want to yell, "You're disgusting! Can't you finger each other in the back of the bus like the rest of us?"

I hate pretending to like the afterglow of love. You know, that special moment when the sex act is finished and you're sweating like Roman Polanski at a Girl Scout jamboree and wondering if you're going to have genital warts in the morning? What *are* you supposed to do when you're done making love? Some people like to smoke, some people like to eat . . . I like to clean under my nails to get rid of any signs of a struggle.

The only thing worse than the afterglow is the cuddling. It's annoying. You crushed my pelvis, chafed my thighs and ruined my sheets. Why would I want to hug you? You got on, you got off, now get out.

I hate people who say, "There's someone for everyone." There's not. Do you *really* think there was a "special someone" for the Elephant Man? Do you believe that somewhere in the moors lived a nubile, raven-haired beauty who longed for a smelly, pus-oozing, deformed man with greasy hair and an English accent? Don't be stupid. He could've been hung like a hippopotamus and it wouldn't have mattered. Even ugly girls have a limit. Trust me, if he was getting his cockney sucked, he was paying for it.

I hate it when ridiculously mismatched couples think their relationship is based on love. Believe me, one of them knows it ain't. Case in point, Hugh Hefner and Miss May . . . That's not a May–December romance; that's a Miss May–Please-God-may-he-not-live-to-December romance. And I hate it when the hot runway model with the 38Ds is "dating" an eighty-seven-year-old man with a catheter and early dementia and she says, "My Bobbykins is so smart and funny. I love him." Her Bobbykins is drooling onto his tie. Believe me, he doesn't make her wet. The *only* person he's making wet is himself. And the only thing she wants to get out of Bobbykins's pants is his wallet.

And I hate the naïve people who look at them and say, "She adores him. She talks to him all the time." You know what she's saying? "Sign here, sweetheart, it's okay."

I hate having to play along with the happy May–December couple lie. It's exhausting. One time I was at a book party in the Hamptons and into the soiree comes Bambi the Bimbo, pushing her boyfriend, Methuselah Finklestein (of the Five Towns Finklesteins), across the room in his wheelchair. She's eleven, he's a hundred and two and I'm supposed to act like it's a perfectly normal relationship and that all blond Russian supermodels with slight overbites fall madly in love with wrinkled, liver-spotted, half-deaf pieces of petrified wood. Believe me, it wasn't easy making conversation that they could both be involved in, but thank God I finally came up with, "Are you two wearing matching MedicAlert bracelets? That is so sweet."

I hate it when people introduce you to someone and use the word "lover." What *lover* means is, "I ingest this person's bodily fluids." *Yuuuccck.* Do I really need to have that image in my head two seconds after we're introduced? "Hi, I'm Jeffrey and this is my lover, Nathan, and I consider his semen to be one of the four basic food groups." Or "I'm Bob and this is my lover, Susie, and I use her vaginal secretions as an emollient." This is too much information for an internist, let alone an aging yenta like me.

To me, "we're lovers" means (a) they're a pair of wussies who are afraid of commitment, or (b) there's something seriously wrong with each one of them (seborrhea, erectile dysfunction, hears voices) and the other one is simply waiting for a new trick to come along before hitting the road.

The only thing more annoying than the word *lover* is the recently divorced dentist with the ponytail who stays in the back of his cousin's house in the Hamptons (north of the highway) and introduces you to "my lady." I usually just throw up right on him.

I was in a nightclub in Camden, New Jersey, and I was in a bad mood. The opening act was a magician/gynecologist whose big trick was pulling a hat out of a rabbit. Anyhow, a guy comes into my dressing room and says, "I'd like you to meet my lady." I said, "When were you knighted?"

I hate the term "partner." "Yes, we're partners . . . This is my life partner, Teddy." Jacoby & Meyers are partners. Ben & Jerry are partners. Bausch + Lomb are partners. You and Teddy are fuck-buddies.

I hate weddings. Weddings are nothing more than catering with virgins. Sorry, in the old days it was virgins; now it's baby mommas.

I hate when they throw rice. If you want to throw rice put the children of Darfur on the guest list.

I hate Viennese tables. The only Viennese people I've ever heard of were Sigmund Freud, Adolf Hitler and the von Trapp Family Singers—and from what I'm told they all hated fancy desserts, not to mention black-tie affairs and hors d'oeuvres. (And speaking of hors d'oeuvres, never serve pigs in a blanket at a bris. It's just wrong. Oh, and never call them *pigs in a blanket.* Use the classy term: *pork in a duvet.*)

I hate fat brides. A fat girl in a white satin gown doesn't look beautiful; she looks like an avalanche. I went to a fat girl wedding once. First they threw rice and then, in honor of the bride, they threw gravy. She was so fat there was only room on the cake for one. The priest said, "I now pronounce you husband and Pantload." He gave her the wafer, she put Velveeta on it and swallowed.

And I hate it when fat girls don't own up to their fatness. They say things like, "I have a slow metabolism" or "It's a glandular condition." Hey, tubby! The tongue is not a gland. Put the cake down.

You know what's worse than a fat bride? A pregnant bride. Pregnant brides should not wear white. They should wear oversized T-shirts that read: I'M A BIG WHORE. Instead of "Here Comes the Bride," when she walks down the aisle they should play, "I'm Easy."

I also hate ugly brides. I went to one wedding where the bride was so hideous I heard *her* mother whisper to the groom, "Don't be a schmuck. Take the maid of honor. It's not too late." Her father was in such a hurry to get her married he tried to give her away on the way to the church.

I hate WASP weddings. There's never enough food. As a Jew, can I just say that petit fours and gin do not a meal make? Protestants don't eat at weddings. They drink and make fun of the Jewish guests who are rifling through the pantries looking for sustenance.

I hate "dry" weddings where they don't serve alcohol. If I want dry, I'll spend time in the Mojave Desert or take pictures of my vagina.

There's this new wedding trend called "destination weddings." I hate them. This is where the stupid—I mean happy couple gets married on some far-off island and expects you to fly yourself there and put yourself up, in addition to bringing a gift and pretending that you give a shit about them. The invitation always gives you "suggestions" as to where to stay. You have three choices of hotels: For $1,000 per night you get a room with a whirlpool, sauna and automatic mood lighting. For $500 per night you get a view of the ocean and turndown service. And for a buck sixty you can sleep in a locker in the Greyhound terminal, which is so small even the mice are hunchbacked. And you know what? For zero dollars, I can stay home, and you can go fuck yourselves.

I hate weddings with cash bars. Very tacky. The only time you'll see me open my purse is to give the Mexican busboy the key to my room. If they expect me to pay for the booze, then I expect them to pay for the rehab.

I hate gay weddings. I'm thrilled about the equal rights thing, but I really don't want to see my mechanic, Ralph, wearing a white dress with a sweetheart neckline and a train.

Gay weddings are like the War on Terror—they go on forever. No "wham, bam, thank you, Sam." Gay weddings are like a lifetime commitment . . . *for the guests.* They start at seven and they end in October. Why? Because stereotypes be damned, gays love parades, that's why. And a gay wedding is nothing more than a parade with crudités. (One of my gay Jewish friends even threw a parade at his mother's shiva. Instead of mourners there were mummers and the casket was pulled on a huge "salute to whitefish" float.)

I hate lesbian weddings. I never know what to say to the mother. "You're not losing a daughter, you're gaining a carpet muncher" just doesn't seem right. I went to a lesbian wedding recently. One of the brides was butch and the other was fem, yet they both wore gowns. Of course, one of the gowns was satin and one was flannel . . . and did you know that Timberland had a bridesmaids line? I didn't.

It was a gorgeous affair. Everything was done in pink and white. There was an ice sculpture of Rosie O'Donnell and gift bags from Home Depot. . . . And the catering? *C'est magnifique!*—salmon, trout, halibut, bass, scallops, shrimp, tuna. All fantastic. The only thing I didn't like was the dessert. They served ladyfingers and even with an entire bottle of Moët and a shot of Irish coffee, I just couldn't.

My favorite moment was when the Universal Life minister,* an unfortunate-looking woman named Lotus, who had Medusa-like hair and chin stubble, pronounced them married and the brides exchanged kisses. Some of the guests thought it was poetic and some of them thought it was awkward. And the straight guy sitting next to me thought it was hot because "Who doesn't like a little girl-on-girl action?"

I hate interfaith marriages. Melissa's friend, David Levyschwartzberg, married a German girl, Fraulein Helga Bunker. She wasn't European or Prussian, she was German! It was a horror. Instead of a veil, Helga wore a helmet. Her wedding song was *"Deutsch-*

---

*All lesbian weddings have Universal Life ministers—it's some kind of a rule. Gay men like to have priests and I say, "Why not?" They've been sleeping with them for years.

land Uber Alles." The limo she came in had a sidecar. And the wedding gown, *uggh!* The train was filled with people. Above the door to the bridal suite was a sign that read, *"Arbeit macht frei."*

What I do love about weddings is reading the announcements in the *New York Times*. It's the highlight of my Sunday. I read the wedding announcements in a very specific order: First I check out the gay couples. The lesbians always have jobs like "professor of women's studies" or "postal supervisor" or "soccer coach." And the gay men are always eight hundred years old because they've been together since 1972 but just got the right to be married in 2011. And I look at their pictures and think, *You waited all these years so you could fuck* that?

And then I check out the interracial couples and play the Which Family Is More Disappointed? game. And if I see a really old, moneyed WASP marrying an inner-city black woman, my heart skips a beat:

Preston Riley Wadsworth Johnson III of Locust Valley and Palm Beach is set to marry Lashonda Taniqua Makisha Washington of 144th Street near the C train. The groom is the senior vice president of acquisitions at Goldman Sachs; the bride doesn't do shit. The wedding is scheduled for some time in early November or maybe late October if Lashonda can get time knocked off for good behavior. The groom is the son of the late Mr. and Mrs. Preston

Johnson II, who died in a suicide pact eight days ago. The bride is the daughter of Diaphonous Marvella Jones and either Marvin Lewis, Eugene Martin or JoJo Murphy.

But the best, best, best thing I like about weddings is the sex. Because once you get married, you don't have to have it anymore.

BAD IDEAS FOR
FIRST DATE MOVIES

Schindler's List

Unless you have a fetish about huddled, starving factory workers making pots and pans, this is a boner-killer.

Caligula

Forty minutes into this three-hour movie, Caligula is screwing
a horse. No amount of hand-holding or coy snuggling will get
you through this evening.

Marley & Me

It's really just *Old Yeller* with a wrinkled Jennifer Aniston. Only
in this film, the wrong dog dies.

Psycho

So much for the cutesy-poo postcoital shower.

Titanic

If Kate Winslet had dropped twenty pounds, maybe the fucking
boat wouldn't have sunk.

The Sound of Music

This is the story of a family of musical children who hide in a cemetery to avoid the Nazis and then run away with a soldier and a nun . . . are you moist yet?

The Accused

Unless you love pool, or you find the prospects of Jodie Foster with a man stimulating, this is not a date flick.

Jaws

You'll never want oral sex again.

The Wizard of Oz

I know, you're thinking, *But everyone loves* The Wizard of Oz. But not for a first date. Judy Garland and thousands of midgets? Please.

MANNERS

Amy Vanderbilt
July 22, 1908–December 27, 1974.
Suicide. Vanderbilt was an American
authority on etiquette. In 1952, she
published the bestselling book
*Amy Vanderbilt's Complete Book
of Etiquette.*

Everyone knows that Amy Vanderbilt died by
jumping out of a window. What everyone
doesn't know is that she put a doily on the
sidewalk before she jumped.

She was a lady till the end.

■

I fucking hate that people are crude and don't have manners anymore. The last time a man leaned over and opened a car door for me we were on the freeway, and the last time a man pulled out a chair for me I was in Aspen and we were on a ski lift. Maybe I'm old fashioned, but I believe when a woman enters a room, men should stand up—and gay men should stand up at least halfway.

Manners matter. For all of his failings, Kadafi had a "please" and "thank-you" for everyone. Idi Amin sent lovely notes after every dinner, cannibal *or* vegetarian. Ted Bundy *always* opened the car door for those girls. As busy as they were, if those men could find the time for etiquette, so can you.

I grew up with a guy who, to this day, has the worst manners of any human I've ever seen. People were so repulsed by his lack of decorum they'd stop him and say, "My God, you must've been raised by wolves!" And he'd say, "Yes, I was." His name was Henry Wolf (technically he was raised by the Wolfs, but why nitpick?) They lived down the hall in apartment 9J. Let me tell you, the Wolfs were pigs. Roaches took a look at their kitchen and committed suicide.

I hate bad table manners. For example, according to etiquette, you're always supposed to leave something on your plate. Unlike Kirstie Alley, who doesn't even leave the pattern. And never, ever put your elbows on the table. If you do then you can't free up your hands to smack the whiny little brats sitting next to you—or grope your best friend's husband.

I hate people who chew with their mouths open. Chewing is the start of the digestive process and I don't want to watch it. If I want to see a foreign object in someone's mouth I'll look at Colin Farrell's sex tape. I don't want to witness the beginning of the process any more than I do its end. It's food, not feed; you're a person, not an animal, so unless you go to a restaurant where they serve cud, unless your name is Elsie and you have an endorsement deal with Borden's, zip your lips. As I tell my grandson and all his little friends, "Children, if you're chewing, your mouth shouldn't be open wider than your mommy's legs when the FedEx man visits."

I hate people who talk with food in their mouth. Don't do it!!! You're not interesting enough that whatever it is you're going to tell me can't wait until you swallow.

Let's say you're an accountant or an actuary and we meet at a cocktail party. (Okay, the odds of that aren't good, what with my being beyond famous, a great diva, a fashion icon and ambassador to five third-world countries and you being, well, an actuary, but for the purpose of this book let's say we do meet). We're having canapés and hors d'oeuvres—maybe lump crab or mushroom caps or, if it's a Hasidic event, something overcooked and bland. Anyway, you shove a deviled egg into your puss and immediately start whining about balance sheets or nose hair or basketball, and I'm standing there, bored and nauseous, dodging bits of yolk. How is this okay? No one, and I mean no one (unless they can help my career), is fascinating enough to start a conversation when they have a mouthful of chopped liver. So unless you're going to warn me that Freddy Krueger is sneaking up behind me with an ax, finish chewing first.

I hate people who make sucking sounds with their teeth. It's both vulgar and mystifying at the same time. What have they got stuck between their teeth that tastes so good? Certainly nothing I cooked.

If a person has something stuck in his teeth, tell him! You can say things like, "Bet that meal was good. I see you're saving some for later." Or "I'm glad to see you're not one of those people who feels compelled to brush."

I hate double-dippers, those inconsiderate slobs who put their crackers in the dip, take a bite, and then dip in again. That is so disgusting. Now the hummus is contaminated—like the Ohio River or Courtney Love's bloodstream.

I hate people who blow their nose at the dinner table and then look in their hankie. What do they think they're going to find? "Look, I just blew out Jimmy Hoffa . . . and he's covered in snot!"

I hate nose picking, especially in restaurants. It's a disgusting habit, but as it turns out, a prerequisite to getting a job as a cabdriver in New York City. I know sometimes you have to remove something from your nose—mucus, dried phlegm, or just part of your old nose—but once you've finished the excavation please don't flick it or wipe it on your napkin. There's a reason God gave the woman at the next table dolman sleeves.

I hate people who belch. In Japan, burping is the sign of a good meal, but in America it's a sign that someone needs a good antacid. I used to have a business friend* who burped at the end of every meal and then said, "You know, in Tokyo that's considered a

---

*Business friend: Someone you wouldn't spit on if he were not in a position to help you make lots of money.

compliment!" So I went to his house and shit on the table and said, "In Libya that means you're rich enough to eat."

I hate people who don't use silverware. Unless you're in Morocco or Ethiopia, do not eat with your hands. In Morocco they eat *everything* with their hands, which makes it very difficult to enjoy soup (although it is a lot of laughs watching them eat pudding). Ethiopia's a little better because they have nothing to eat. So while their stomachs may be bloated, their fingers are squeaky clean.

I hate men who don't pull out a lady's chair at the table. Unless it's a wheelchair. Yes, watching a helpless paralytic wriggle around on the carpet sure is funny, but helping her back into her chair is a huge pain in the ass. I'm a giver, but I don't lift. And since I'm on the topic: Can we talk about handicapped etiquette?

I hate the handicapped and their privileged parking. Why should the lame be able to park close to the mall entrance while I have to schlep through the rain and the wind and the sleet to do my shopping? Dollars to donuts I'm going to spend more than they will. How many pairs of crutches does one need, or reflector lights or stick-on rails for the bathroom?

I hate people who decorate their wheelchairs with flags and stickers and tinsel and horns and feathers. You're a paraplegic, not a mummer. I find that kind of "look at me" narcissism terribly inconsiderate. If you need attention that badly, set yourself on fire.

I hate dealing with the handicapped as I never know the proper etiquette. What am I supposed to do when I'm introduced to someone who has tiny thalidomide hands? Nod affectionately and say, "You know, *Flipper* was one of my favorite shows"? Or do I go with something kicky like, "I can see who's the swimmer in your family"?

I hate that it's my responsibility to know which ear is your "good" ear. I start talking and five minutes into telling some hilarious story about Tom Cruise and a thermometer you interrupt with, "Could you please speak into my good ear?" So not only have I lost my punch line because you broke the rhythm, but I'm also aggravated because you wasted five minutes of my valuable time—time that could have been better spent shopping or berating others. So unless you're Vincent van Gogh, wear a sign that reads: TRY THE LEFT EAR. THE RIGHT ONE'S JUST FOR SHOW.

I hate handicapped ramps in sidewalks. They create puddles and are so filled with wheelchair people it's hard to skateboard down them.

I hate the rules about Seeing Eye dogs or "companion animals."* The disabled can be so fussy. If you encounter a Seeing Eye dog on the street you're not supposed to pet them or scratch them or even say "Stop" when they lead their master into oncoming traffic.

I hate having to look the blind in the eye. It makes me very self-conscious and I don't do self-conscious well. I remember the good old days when blind people wore sunglasses and gently rocked back and forth when speaking, like they were davening in temple. That all changed when José Felícíano got too big for his britches. In the late sixties José had a nice little career going: He had a couple of hit songs, wore a macramé plant holder on his head and was a regular on *The Ed Sullivan Show.* (FYI, on Sullivan, José was always preset, like the Austrian plate spinners or Topo Gigio, so he wouldn't wander the stage for a half hour, feeling for his mark with his shoe.) Anyway, somewhere between "Light My Fire" and "Feliz Navidad" José got the bright idea that his fans wanted to see his eyes when he sang. Wrong. We didn't. If I'm interested in seeing two balls bouncing around someone's face I'll sneak into George Michael's bedroom.

And to finish off the subject of blind people: They have no social manners. When was the last time a blind

---

*Exactly what is a "companion animal"? A goat you've been fucking for ten years but refuse to marry for tax purposes?

person paid you a compliment, like, "Hey, you've lost weight!" or "Wow, fuckface, you sure have gotten old."

I hate people who cross the street against the light. I think drivers should be allowed to run them over. The notion that they're so important that everyone else on the road has to stop short, thus throwing the kids through the windshield, is ridiculous. Okay, maybe the "kids through the windshield" thing isn't so bad, but still, why should we have to ruin our brake pads because some asshole can't tell "stop" from "go?"

Even the aforementioned blind have no excuse to cross against the light. These days the goddamned walk/don't walk signs beep, whiz, bang and speak. Even Stephen Hawking, blindfolded, would get the message not to wheel into oncoming traffic.

I hate people who can't walk two blocks without drinking water. How thirsty could you be? Did you have a block of salt for lunch? If camels can go months without stopping for a bottle of Poland Spring, surely you can get to Fifty-eighth Street. Anne Frank went almost two years before she needed a little quenching. Helen Keller may have yelled, "Water," but she didn't stick her head under the pump and start slurping. Parched as she was, she went right up to her agent and made a book and movie deal first.

I hate people who offer me a drink of water from their bottle after wiping it off with the

hem of their sweaty T-shirt and then, when I refuse, they won't take "no" for an answer.

"You look like a prune, have a sip."

"No thank you, I'm fine."

"No really, have some, it's good for you."

"No, no . . . I'm hydrogen intolerant."

So what I do now is take a drink and give the bottle back to them. And once they've sipped from it again I say, "Did I tell you that right before I met you here today I blew a homeless guy." They'll never bother you about water again.

I hate people who don't know how to handle a fart in the elevator. If you're the owner of the offending tush and you've let loose something more noxious than Zyklon B and you can't ignore the watering eyes of fellow passengers, then at least have the manners to quietly acknowledge the horror. And while there may be nothing you can say to make restitution for their collapsed lungs, you can certainly try to look apologetic and make an excuse. A surefire one for me is, "I had no idea Michelle Obama's recipe for fried chicken gives you gas. I was just trying to be a good Democrat." The goal here is not to deny ownership of the mushroom cloud but to elicit sympathy from the offended parties, which serves two purposes: (1) They will forgive the flatulence, and (2) It gives you license to fart again and again and again.

I hate people who are too polite. For example, when you're on line for popcorn at the movie theater and the guy behind the counter says, "Next guest." I'm not a guest, you pimple-faced high-school dropout. I'm a customer. You have Jujubes and I'm going to buy them. That's the extent of our relationship. Get it? Guests are people who come to my house for dinner. I don't charge them for the brisket or the soup because they're *guests.* So if you're going to say that I'm a guest then treat me as a guest. Allow me to help myself to the Junior Mints, the nonpareils, some Milk Duds, Chuckles and six bags of Gummi Bears. And if you even think of asking me for a penny I'll clog up your toilets and slash your tires. And worst of all I'll make you sit through a Dane Cook film festival.

I hate people who always find something nice to say about others. My husband, Edgar, was one of those people. I hate that kind of largesse. One day I asked him, "Hey, four-eyes, what about John Wayne Gacy? He killed thirty-three boys and buried them under his house. What nice thing can you say about him?" And Edgar said, "Well, he wasn't lazy. And he was a homeowner!"

I hate people who talk to me from the next stall in public restrooms, especially when— to be blunt—they're moving their bowels! I'm not an English professor, but I am pretty sure grunting isn't part of sentence structure. If you're going to chat me up stall to stall, then the only words coming out of your mouth better be, "Oh my God, I think I lost the fetus!" or "Is this your five-carat diamond ring that just rolled over here?"

I hate hosts who hide the extra roll of toilet paper in their guest bathrooms. When I have guests, I don't hide the toilet paper. I want them to know where it is. Or at least know where I can find a good dry cleaner for the drapes they used instead.

Why do hostesses always hide the extra roll of toilet paper in some kind of a knitted cozy thing that looks like an upside down cap? Is this just a passive-aggressive way of saying, "Go shit in your hat?"

If you're a guest at a dinner party and want to leave the powder room smelling daisy fresh, always carry matches or a little spray with you, just in case. If you're a vegan, please carry an industrial pesticide, like DDT. Otherwise you'll have to hide in the bathroom for twenty minutes to let the place aerate. Pretend you're the quality-control manager at a sulfur mine.

I hate guests who don't tell you they have special dietary needs. If you're kosher or halal or vegetarian or lactose intolerant or just tend to vomit up most cooked foods, don't be angry with me because I won't cook something special for you. (All that defrosting wears me out.) What I will do is have one of my many illegal staff members do it. I find people are willing to do all kinds of things with the threat of deportation hanging over their heads.

I threw a fabulous dinner party once for a well-known actor who shall remain nameless: Matthew Modine. He arrived and said, "My wife's a vegan. She doesn't eat anything with eyes." I said, "You must have a shitty sex life."

I hate guests who kiss me when I'm hosting a party. When you come in, say "hello," give me an air kiss and go mingle. I have no idea where your mouth has been. I don't want you to give me a big kiss and then for the rest of the evening I have this lingering taste of Fleet Week in my mouth.

I hate guests who can't make conversation. If you accept an invitation to a party you have an obligation to be ready to converse. My good friend, well, friend . . . well, acquaintance . . . okay, Barbara Walters says you should always have four good stories to tell at a cocktail party. I say three will do, but only if all three of them involve major celebrities who have had explosive colitis in public places.

I hate people who don't turn off their cell phones at parties because there's always some ass who will call you. In my case it's the pope. The man doesn't leave me alone. How many times do I have to hear the excuse, "Joan, we *all* had to join the Hitler

Youth, it wasn't a choice; if it was up to me I would have joined B'nai B'rith."

I hate people who are early to parties. I think of them as premature *conversators*. (And yes, I know "conversators" is not a word; I'm just pandering to an urban demographic.) If I invite you to dinner at seven and you arrive wildly early, let's say six fifty-nine, I may still be getting dressed, doing my hair or having a face-lift. So before accepting an invite, learn to tell time.

I hate people who don't know when to leave the party. If you don't have a mild case of Asperger's syndrome, you have no excuse to not pick up the social cues that it's time to leave. Simple things like the food is all gone, or the servants have finished cleaning and are back in the basement tied to the radiators, or I'm upstairs in my bra and panties, rinsing my falsies and waxing my legs. Pay attention. Get out.

I hate people who think their medical condition is table talk. Do not show up at an event with any postoperative wounds that require changing. If you reek of salve, stay home.

I hate people who don't listen or pay attention. When an invitation says, "No gifts, please," that means, "No gifts, please." If you're not a member of the FBI, the CIA, the NSA, the Stasi or the Penn State football team, chances are no one is speaking to you in some secret code that can only be cracked by an enigma machine. I'm specific when I send out an invitation, so if you bring me a gift when I asked you not to, I'm now in the position of having to scrounge around to find *you* a gift. And that's a horrible position to be in—almost as bad as double penetration. What am I going to find to give you, an old bra? "That belonged to Marilyn Monroe! Look! One of Joe DiMaggio's pubic hairs is still caught in the underwire!"

I hate people who bring lousy gifts to a party.

A gift is supposed to be a nice gesture, not a showstopper. Candles, coffee-table books and French chocolates are lovely ideas—and I can re-gift them before you even sit down. Here are some things *not* to give a hostess:

- A litter of piglets
- An ugly orphan (It's hard enough to love even the pretty ones; don't bring me Mr. Uggo.)
- Memory albums (You say, "Let's look at this together!" I say, "Let's pretend we have Alzheimer's and not waste the time.")
- Crabs or any other communicable disease
- Cheap wine (Unless the hostess is a moron, in which case it's okay. "Vintage, four o'clock? Why, that was a very good time.")
- A vibrator (Very tough to re-gift—even if you wash it.)

Never buy gifts on sale. The late Dinah Shore used to do this and it ruined her reputation. She spent years building up her street cred by schtupping Burt Reynolds but threw it all away buying cheap schlock and trying to pass it off as high-end. Dinah would buy some crappy piece of dreck then put it in a Saks bag and give it as a gift. She did it to me once and I said, "Dinah, Saks doesn't sell toaster ovens!" I don't mean to trash Dinah Shore, but she's dead; she can't sue me, so fuck her.

I never bring a gift to party. I sneak into the hostess's bedroom and add my name to cards.

The worst gifts of all time were bought by the three wise men: frankincense, gold and myrrh. Frankincense is just a candle and not even the good kind like they sell on QVC. Gold is okay but make sure it's real gold. If I bite it and its chocolate I'm not going to be happy. And myrrh is an anal lubricant. Which makes perfect sense . . . three men, all alone in the desert.

I hate people who go to the movies and act like they're watching Netflix in their den. (And FYI, I say "den" and not family room because the only room the entire family should ever be in together is the lobby in Gutterman's chapel after an unexpected yet thrilling death of a rich, semi-loved one.) Here are some basic movie theater rules:

1. Shut the fuck up. I didn't pay eight bucks to listen to you. If I want to hear what you have to say I'll swing by your house for some coffee and babka. I'm

in show business so I'm pretty sure that nowhere in the script did the writer or director say, ". . . and then Barry, in the ninth row, chimes in . . ."

    a. If the movie has to be explained to you as it's going along, then you're too stupid to be in a theater with other people. This is especially true if you're watching the Zapruder film.

    b. Don't keep saying, "What did he say? What did he say?" You may be deaf but I'm not. And don't sit there and fiddle with your Miracle-Ear, either. Not only is the fidgeting annoying, but the damned thing buzzes and vibrates. If I'm in a dark theater and something is buzzing it better be between my legs, not in your ears.

2. Don't crinkle cellophane. There are only a few sounds more annoying than candy bars being *sloooowwwwly* unwrapped—a baby crying, a dog yelping, Yoko Ono singing—so unwrap your Chuckles the way you'd pull gauze off a third-degree burn—bite down on a sock and yank quickly.

3. Don't text message! If I'm in a dark room and I see a white light, I think it's the light at the end of the tunnel and I'm dying. And kicking the shit out of you is on my bucket list. So don't be stupid; turn off your smart-phone.

4. If you're late to a movie, don't stand in the aisle hovering over me looking for a prime location. Just put your fat ass in the first seat you find. Unless that seat is next to me, in which case I suggest you go fuck yourself and sit behind the screen.

5. Unless you're at a private screening in the director's house, don't clap at the end of the movie. The actors can't hear you; they're not in the theater—they're in rehab.

6. When the movie's over don't stand up and linger and block the screen so I can't see the credits. You may not care who the key grip on the Zimbabwe shoot was, but I do. A lot of those sons of bitches owe me money.

I hate road rage. Road rage is all the rage, but it need not be that way. If people had basic car manners the world would be a much safer place; not nearly as interesting—be honest, you don't get just a little moist thinking about a six-car pileup?—but safer.

I hate people who honk their horns incessantly for no apparent reason. Traffic, slowpokes and the old lady looking through the steering wheel with her blinker on for two hundred miles create frustration, for sure. But none of them are reasons to hit the horn; they are reasons to hit the bottle. No, no, no, I'm not encouraging drinking and driving (I don't want to get those crazy lezzies in MADD angry at me), but honestly, if you've got a buzz on, the sound of the horn will give you a headache so you'll be *less* inclined to beep.

I hate people who have sex in the backseat while I'm driving. It's not only rude; it's exclusionary. Also, if you're going to give a blow job in a car—swallow! You don't want to ruin the fine Corinthian leather.*

I hate people who decorate their cars. I don't want a bobblehead dog or a forlorn, bloody Jesus staring at me. Even worse, I don't want to see pictures of your kids. Why do you have to have photos of Jimmy and Kenny taped to your dashboard? You saw them at breakfast a half hour ago; how much could you miss them? Even Jerry Sandusky doesn't do that, and he really likes kids.

I love games you can play on road trips. Here's a good road game: If you're driving in front of a motorcycle, slow down and throw coffee out your window directly into the motorcyclist's face. His skid marks will go for miles. This is even more fun on a side street when you're driving in front of a bicycle. You can take out the bike, the kid, a hydrant, a tree and, if you're lucky, a cat.

Want some fun for the whole family? Push the dog

---

*A tip to dieters: Be aware of the caloric intake involved here. According to the *New York Times,* one teaspoon of sperm contains 148 calories, or if you're in Weight Watchers, two points.

out the window and speed off and then place bets on how long Fido will chase the car before he collapses. Sounds cruel on paper, but trust me, this is a great, fun way to reunite a dysfunctional family.

And by the way, **I hate people who have a giant dog and let him hang his head out the window.** They think of it as fun for their bullmastiff. I think of it as nothing more than a bull's-eye.

I hate people who don't understand funeral etiquette. A display of bad manners can really screw up a fun shiva or a merry wake.

For example, you should never ask the widow about the cause of death; you should know that before you show up at her door. However, if you hate the widow, then by all means bring it up. "Is it true they found Norman just like David Carradine, hanging naked from a shower rod, wearing a horse collar and butt plug?"

If the widow offers up the cause of death, then it's perfectly acceptable to dive right into the conversation headfirst. "Jerry died of natural causes." "How do you define 'natural'? Were any livestock involved? Jerry was a cutter, no?"

I hate people who say, "At least he didn't suffer." Maybe he did, you don't know. For some people, a prolonged illness is considered suffering. For others, sitting through a Ben Stiller movie marathon is torture. One man's pain is another man's weakness. Don't judge.

I hate when people use euphemisms, such as "My Ralphie passed this morning." No, he didn't. He's dead. He's not passing anything. He can't move, that's the whole point, you idiot. He's lying there like a big lump.

I hate boring funerals. Funerals are so boring. I like to play games to liven things up, games like Who's Next? I like to make it every tenth person; trust me, it'll get you giggling and the hours will fly. Pull My Finger is another terrific picker-upper. Go right up to the widow and say it. Guaranteed to make you feel good, especially if her Herman died of gastritis.

Always make a joke when looking in the casket, and say it loud enough to be heard over the sobbing. Some good things to say are: "What's that green shit stuck in his teeth?" or "Guess who's got a boner?" And my favorite is, "Oops, that's not Liza Minnelli. Wrong funeral, sorry!"

I hate people who smirk or make comments during the eulogy. Rolling your eyes should be more than enough.

I hate people who don't know how long to stay at a condolence call. Five minutes is too short. That says either you didn't really care about the deceased or the family or you have something more important to do. (This is especially rude if you're carrying a bowling ball or fishing tackle.) Rule number one: The amount of time you spend paying respects is directly proportionate to the amount of money you've been left in the will. If it's more than six figures, bring a cot to the chapel and move the fuck in.

Seating at a funeral is important. The front rows are usually reserved for family and lifelong friends. However, if you're like me and you dressed up, took a cab and canceled a pedicure, then you want to be seen. Look, I know little Susie is missing Daddy, but I'm in Valentino, so let's get our priorities straight. She'll miss him forever but this dress will be out of style by September. . . . I'm sitting up front. And FYI, a quick fashion note: Just because wearing black is no longer a requirement at funerals, you should still try to look decent. You should never, ever wear flip-flops, capri pants or a T-shirt that reads: LET GO OF MY EARS, I KNOW WHAT I'M DOING.

Which brings up the next thing: No hugging or touching. I hate widows, especially the sloppy kind. We all liked Bernie, but I don't want mucus on my mink.

I hate people who bring flowers when the family has requested either no flowers or "in lieu of . . ." The most appropriate gift is a donation to the person's favorite charity, or their alma mater, or the Bunny Ranch if that's where he spent most of his free time.

And finally, it is always good manners to send a note or card offering condolences. Amy Vanderbilt sent out 237 individual suicide notes. All in calligraphy. I'll say it again: a lady till the end.

EXCUSES

My favorite excuses to cover gaffes, mistakes or hideous faux pas:

▶ *I'm a widow.*

The more recent, the better. Here's how it goes . . .

You: "I'm sorry I sat on your priceless Ming vase. I'm a widow."

Host: "Oh, how terrible, when did your husband die?"

You: (pause, look at watch) "Three o'clock."

Host: "And you're *here*?"

You: "One has to push on; I couldn't miss your party."

▶ *I lost a child.*

Is there anything worse than losing a child? Yes, losing two or three. Unless of course you're the Octomom, in which case that would just be considered thinning the herd. This is an excuse you can only use under the direst of circumstances, i.e., you gave military secrets to an enemy or threw up on Oprah, or wore orange to a black-and-white ball.

▶ *I survived 9/11.*

This is the perfect excuse for everyone. "I'm sorry I sideswiped your Mercedes. I survived 9/11." You don't have to have been in the Towers, or even known anyone in the Towers. You don't have to be a New Yorker or even an American. You could simply be someone who was alive that day and the excuse still holds water: The trauma of the day is still so intense that no one questions you.

▶ *The Holocaust.*

9/11 with striped pajamas. "I lost my entire family at Auschwitz." You don't have to add, "We got separated in the gift shop."

▶ *I was raped when I was in college.*

Other than me, what kind of person is going to snoop to verify your claim? Medical and academic records are private. This excuse really only works if you graduated during the last ten years. After fifty, no one wants to think of you in any sexual situation whatsoever, and will not be sympathetic to you. "Raped? By whom, the Comanches?"

▶ *My father beat my mother.*

Is there anything more traumatic than watching your father beat your mother? Yes . . . watching your mother beat your father. Ladies and gentlemen, I give you David Gest and Liza Minnelli. When Gest filed for divorce he claimed Liza used to beat him up. How is that possible? Liza Minnelli doesn't have the strength to beat an egg or a drug habit, yet she was able to kick his ass up and down Christopher Street??? Please.

▶ *I just found out my brother is my father.*

This excuse is best used in the Deep South, Utah or Mackenzie Phillips's house.

► **I was forced into being a sex slave.**

You're only a slave if you didn't get a back-end distribution deal.

► **PTSD.**

Not unlike the 9/11 excuse-mongers, you don't have to have been in an actual war to claim post-traumatic stress disorder. Simply having seen Marlon Brando in a loincloth in the jungle in *Apocalypse Now* is more than enough of a shock to keep this tidy little excuse in your back pocket.

► **I sometimes hear voices.**

This implies the voices just might come back, and they might come back *now*, while you are shaming me and making me feel bad about myself because I didn't send a thank-you note for your stupid e-card. No social miscue is worth that kind of risk. (What I don't add is that although usually when people hear "voices," those voices tell them to kill passersby or to go on shooting sprees in Southern malls and fast-food restaurants, my voices say, *Hurry over to Bergdorf's for their amazing mid-winter fur sale.*)

EAT ME!

If God wanted me to cook, my hands would be made of aluminum.

■

I live in New York City where there are probably five million apartments and I believe only eleven of them actually have kitchens. New Yorkers don't cook. We order in, or we go out. The only things New Yorkers put in the oven are their heads.

I consider cooking to be one of the true wonders of the world, like the great pyramids of Giza or the Hanging Gardens of Babylon or the unexplained success of Carrot Top. I've never been much of a cook; in fact when Melissa was born I had one of my neighbors breast-feed her. I told her to think of it as "ordering in."

But I *have* eaten in restaurants and homes all over the world, from Buckingham Palace to White Castle, and whether it's a five-star or a drive-thru, I can always find something to complain about.

Question: What's the most important thing for a restaurant?

Answer: Location, location, location.

Most major cities have ethnic neighborhoods and ethnic restaurants. In Los Angeles, you can go to Koreatown; in Detroit, get in your car and go to Greektown; in Miami, it's Little Havana; in San Francisco, it's Chinatown; in New York, it's Little Italy. You know what I hate? There is not one city or town where you can just hop in your car and say to the kids, "Let's go to Jewville; we'll get some derma and some heartburn."

I hate maître d's. They're just ushers with control issues. And the first thing you see when you walk into a restaurant, at least in a restaurant that's good enough that the Heimlich maneuver instructions aren't taped to the front door, is the maître d'. You show up at some fancy restaurant at four o'clock in the afternoon on a hot Tuesday in August; the place is so empty (there's more activity in Jessica Simpson's head), the maître d's reservation book is so white he's getting snow-blind. And yet he says, "Do you have reservations?" No, do you think you could squeeze us in before that horrible 4:05 rush? And then, after he spends twenty minutes looking through his empty list, you slip him a sawbuck and he gets all friendly and sweet. I hate that.

He says in this very condescending tone, "How are we, tonight?" I always want to say, "*We're* a little gassy. Come close and take a sniff. How are *you*?"

Fortunately, through the years I've learned there are ways to get back at snotty maître d's. First, after they seat you, complain about the draft and make them move you to a warmer spot. Then, a half hour later, tell them it's a little stuffy and ask to be moved back to the original table. Second, if the kitchen closes at eleven o'clock put in a huge order at ten fifty-eight. And third, linger. When you see the maître d' wants to close down the restaurant and go home, dawdle over your dessert. Drag it out as long as you can. Pretend you're having a romantic moment with your dining partner, even if your dining partner is your brother. And if you really do have to leave, send a note and a fifty dollar bill to another table and ask that couple to chew slower than Chris Christie jogs; make that motherfucker work late.

I hate politically correct jerks who whine that the words *waiter* and *waitress* are pejoratives. The PC storm troopers insist that waiters and waitresses now be called "servers." According to them it's because they're "serving." I say, "Fuck them." *I'm* waiting—for my food.

I don't think waiters and waitresses really care what you call them as long as you tip well. If I was a waitress and I knew there was twenty-five percent coming at the end of the meal, you could call me "Joan Rivers, dog-fucking terrorist child molester" and I'd say, "Thank you, come again!"

I also hate waiters who introduce themselves.
"Hi, I'm Steven. I'll be your server tonight." "Hi, Steven, I'm Joan, and I don't give a shit! Just bring me my Caesar salad and shut up."

The waiter's job is to bring me food from the kitchen; my job is to eat it (or at least push it around the plate and pretend to eat it, like all of those anorexics in Hollywood do). That's going to be the extent of our relationship. We're not going to become BFFs or have pajama parties or spend a crazy weekend on Mykonos together.

But if we *were* going to be pals, then I'd need a lot more information than just a name. "My name is John" simply doesn't cut it. John who? John Foster Dulles? John Philip Sousa? John Wayne Gacy? I vet my friends. I'm like a dog sniffing a hydrant; I know everything about them and their parents and their parents' parents. So if Johnny in the apron wants to be friends, I'll need to know a couple of things, like where he's from, did he go to college, did he go to prison, does he have a girlfriend, does he have money, does he have a will, am I in it?

I hate it when the waiter comes to the table and asks, "Would you like to see a menu?"
What's the correct response to that question: "No. Let me guess what you have in the refrigerator." Or "No, I'm not worthy. I'll just eat the crumbs off of the lap of the old lady at table seven."

I hate it when the waiter reads the daily specials like he's Meryl Streep in *Sophie's Choice*. (And by the by, Sophie made a terrible choice. She should have given the Nazis both of those overacting kids.) The waiter has all the daily specials memorized and he recites them with vigor and gusto and you have no idea what he's talking about and, worse, he has no idea what he's talking about. "Today's entrée special is a *bouquetière* of garden vegetables." You grew up with a prison mom; she didn't serve her parole officer a *bouquetière*, she blew him for a pair of nylons. The other inmates weren't banging their cups and chanting, "We want a *bouquetière*! We want a *bouquetière*!"

And don't come to my table and ask me if I'd like a "festival of roughage." It's a bowl of lettuce and I'm going to shit for a month. Now get away from me and go back in the kitchen.

I hate diners who hound the waiter with ridiculous questions like, "If your mother was eating here tonight, then what would you serve her?" Who knows what his relationship with his mother is like? What if he doesn't like his mother? The last meal Lizzie Borden served her mother was Jell-O and ground gravel. So it's really just a stupid question.

I hate when customers say, "Is that gluten-free? It has to be gluten-free or my throat closes." I was on a plane once and the guy next to me almost died—his throat closed and they had to lay him down in the aisle for the entire flight. I loved it: Finally I had extra leg room. In coach! Since then, every time I travel I carry a tiny bottle of gluten in my purse, just in case I want to stretch out a little.

When I grew up nobody was "gluten-free." Nobody even knew what gluten was. Now everyone's gluten-free, afraid to eat wheat. What a bunch of pussies. Here's an idea: Stay home and have a can of Nine Lives. Stop bothering everybody.

I hate when diners ask, "How is that prepared?" Like the waitresses showed up an hour early to watch the chef cook. Just once I'd like to hear her say, "Well, once the rats are done crapping on it, the chef kicks it across the floor and then I pick it up and reheat it under my armpits."

Equally as annoying is when they ask for substitutions: "Can you replace the mushrooms with olives and replace the bread with fruit and replace the spinach with rice?" I'd love the waiter to say, "How about if I replace your teeth with my fist? Bon appétit!" And . . .

I hate it when people say "bon appétit" in inappropriate places—which would be *any* place other than France. If your salad comes in a plastic container or you're mixing your own coffee or if your entrée is sold by the bucket, don't wink and say, "Bon appétit." Just let me leave quietly, under cover of the night.

I hate men who order wine and like to let it "breathe." You know those types: They put the "f" in pretentious? Every time I see one of them sniff the cork, I have an incredible urge to run over to his table and shove it up his nose.

The asshole sniffs the cork, swirls the wine around his mouth, gargles and then says, "It's bold but not so brash as to overplay the occasion. Do you taste the raspberries? Do you find this wine to have a fascinating woodiness?" I always say, "Yes, I do; just like the inside of a mahogany casket." And then I'd like to water board him with his Chablis.

I hate tipping. After every meal there is the moment when the waiter brings the check to the table. It's for nine dollars and forty-seven cents, you put down a hundred dollar bill and he says, "Would you like some change?"

"Hmm . . . let's see. The bill is nine dollars and forty-seven cents and I gave you a hundred dollar bill. . . . You know what, I don't need any change. I always tip eight thousand percent. And if the ninety-dollar tip isn't enough for you, here are my keys—take the car, let yourself into the house. It's yours. No, really, the service was *that* good. And on your way up the stairs feel free to fuck my sister. She's in the guest room!"

I hate paying cash. I always tip more on a credit card than I do if I'm paying in cash because somehow it feels like I'm spending Visa's money, not my own.

And technically, I'm right because, according to federal law, if you die with a balance on your credit card your family is not obligated to pay it off. Which means that if I have a massive stroke and drop dead right after eating, the last meal was on the house. So I say, "Charge it!" whenever I'm feeling poorly.

I hate it that nowadays *everyone* expects a tip.

In this country, waiters make about a dollar fifty-three an hour, hardly a livable wage, even if you live in Iowa. (I hate it when people come up to me say, "You know, Joan, for what you pay for an apartment in Manhattan, you could have a twelve-bedroom house in Iowa!" That's right, I could. But I'd be in Iowa.)

Tipping isn't an issue in European countries and Australia because waitstaffs are unionized and they're paid decent salaries. They're not working for tips. Which means the service really sucks. I hate that.

But suddenly, everyone expects to be given a gratuity. In the old days delivery boys, hairdressers and the occasional uterus were tipped. Now, everyone expects a reward for "exceptional service." All across America, there are tip jars everywhere. Tip jars are popping up more than Anthony Weiner at a photo shoot.

There are even tip jars on the counters at Baskin-Robbins ice cream stores. Why? There's no kitchen, no table service. It's a scooper, rum raisin and a cone. How exceptional could the service be? Did Billy with the acne make my scoop of vanilla ice cream look like a soft sculpture of Barack Obama? Did he sing the entire score of *Kiss Me, Kate* while putting sprinkles on my cookie? Why should I tip him when he didn't do anything?

I blame the "tipping for no reason syndrome" on Starbucks, who make their customers do all the work. When I go to Starbucks, I'm putting in my own sugar, my own cream, my own straw . . . I might as well go to Columbia with Juan Valdez and get on a donkey and pick the beans. So from here on in, no tips for the "baristas." *Barista* by the way, is an Italian word that means "fucking lazy."

Am I supposed to start tipping everybody, like the usher at the movie theater? How about the guy on the highway crew who waves orange flags to divert traffic? Or my plastic surgeon? Should I leave a twenty on the dresser if he makes my nipples wink?

I hate it when the tables in restaurants are too close together. The only person who likes having strangers on top of him is George Michael in a public toilet.

I don't want other people so close to my table that I can hear them chew, burp and fart. If I want to hear those things, I'll dine alone.

I hate "family restaurants." Next to cheap perfume and vaginal warts it's my least favorite thing. The first time I saw an ad for a "family restaurant" I thought I'd give it a try. Why not, I'm an adventurer, just like Magellan. I thought wrong. The ad said the experience would be "Just like eatin' at home." Sure enough, I sat down and the waitress came over and said, "Put your napkin in your lap, sit up straight, it's a fork, not a shovel, you're fat, you're ugly and your father doesn't touch me anymore."

Then there's "family seating," which is a complete social aberration. Family seating means long picnic tables with dozens of total strangers sitting next to one another chewing. Who does this? Who needs this kind of aggravation? I don't like to have dinner with people I know, let alone a group of strangers that just drove in from Nebraska. Even the Donner Party knew better than to do family seating; they got to the pass, they split up the corpses and then went and ate separately. And you know what? It was a perfectly nice night on the mountain. And no one had to hear strangers' kids complaining, "Knees, again?"

Tasting menus are bullshit. A lot of fancy-schmancy restaurants offer "tasting menus." A tasting menu is when the chef sends out tiny little dollops of his favorite courses for you to taste and charges you three hundred dollars, which is about fifty bucks a dollop. Those dollops, combined, might fill a finger bowl and that's only if you're deformed and have very small, childlike fingers. The biggest problem, other than the cost, is that when you finish the tasting menu you have to go to another restaurant and order a real meal off of their eating menu.

The only thing tasting menus are good for is the

homeless, because the meal never ends. They bring item after item and it goes on and on and on like a Jay Leno monologue. A friend of mine once ordered the tasting menu at a restaurant in L.A.; it took so long that she went through menopause. They started with soup and by the time they got to dessert she was so fucking cranky she had lost her appetite.

I hate restaurants that serve steak tartare.

Steak tartare is a scam. Steak tartare is nothing more than raw chopped meat and onions. Tuna tartare is a can of cat food with pepper. And sushi is just a guppy with rice.

Tartare is considered a delicacy, so it costs a fortune. Explain to me again why should I pay you to *not* cook my food? If I want raw meat I'll take a bite out of a passing Kardashian.

I hate when your food is charged by the weight. It's food, not jewelry. I don't need a three-carat rump roast. The only person in the world whose jewelry and food weighed the same amount was Elizabeth Taylor, and you know where that got her? Forest Lawn Cemetery, that's where.

Fast-food restaurants actually serve things that are *only* sold by their size, like, "the Whopper," "the Double-Double" and the "Quarter Pounder with Cheese." I say, if they're going to offer you meals by the pound the least they could do is offer free angiograms for dessert.

At steak houses they always have two sizes of prime

rib: "the regular" and "the king's portion," which is about half a cow. If you order the smaller portion you look a like a cheapo and if you order the king's portion you look like the self-centered, gluttonous narcissist you are. For me, that's a lose-lose.

I hate lobster houses, too. I hate it when they say, "Pick your lobster." Lobsters are like the Japanese— they all look alike. And just like steak houses, lobster houses serve by size, which I really don't understand because all lobsters weigh about the same amount; they all weigh-in somewhere between one and a half and three pounds. In my entire life I've never once been served an obese nine or ten pound lobster. I don't know how it's possible that every single lobster fits within that narrow weight range, but they do. When it comes to body weight, humans have an enormous bell curve to work with, ranging from Kate Moss on one end to the cast of *The Biggest Loser* on the other.

Yet lobsters are all thin. Did Richard Simmons get them to tone up by releasing a *Working Out with Mollusks* DVD? (Don't kid yourself, if anybody could corner that market, Richard Simmons could. The man is a genius. Back in the day he got kids to work out, he got old people to work out . . . he even got pregnant women to work out—remember that video, *Abortin' to the Oldies*, where you exercise to "Bye, Bye Baby"? Just fantastic, one of my faves

You can't tell me that there are no depressed, overweight female lobsters who sit around the reef in filthy nightgowns eating Fritos and watching *Flipper* reruns.

The other reason I hate lobster houses is that they make you wear a bib. I think that if you have to wear a bib to eat you shouldn't be in a nice restaurant; you should be in assisted living.

I hate children's menus because their presence implies that children are welcome. (See the chapter "For the Children" for more on this.)

Infants should never be allowed in nice restaurants. They smell like dairy cows and they've always got Zwieback crackers stuck in their hair and their parents can't shut them up.

If you want children to be quiet in restaurants, I say change the names of the items on the children's menus. Instead of "The Popeye" or "The Dora the Explorer," the meals should be named things like "The Mommie Dearest" or "The Casey Anthony." I assure you, they'll be quiet.

I hate how chefs dress. What's up with the pants? For no apparent reason every chef, cook or kitchen worker wears grotesque, polyester, black-and-white checkered pants. Is this an ego thing so everyone knows that you're the chef? We know. You're already wearing a giant white hat and you smell like day-old veal.

I hate sitting at a table near the bathroom. I don't want to see the chef coming out, zipping up. The only thing worse than seeing the chef in a restaurant coming out of the men's room is one going in, then stop, say, "Too late," turn around and return to the kitchen.

I hate it when the cook in a diner refers to himself as a "chef." Anthony Bourdain is a chef; Daniel Boulud is a chef; Emeril Lagasse is a chef. But the sweaty guy behind the counter in the diner? That's Nick from Astoria.

I hate people who refer to chocolate cake as "decadent." Sara Lee licking the chocolate off of your thighs is decadent; the cake is just fattening.

I hate restaurants that have drive-thru windows. Unless you're a cult member on a killing spree you shouldn't be able to drive through a restaurant. Remember the nut job who shot up the McDonald's in Texas? My first thought was, *How bad could the onion rings have been?*

I hate McDonald's. I don't want to order dinner by yelling into a plastic clown's mouth. If I want my face in a clown's mouth I'll tongue kiss Glenn Beck.

I hate "Happy Meals." McDonald's seems to think that eating these meals will make you happy. It won't. It may make your cardiologist and his accountant happy, but all it will make you feel is fat and bloated.

If McDonald's wants to make a really happy meal, they ought to make it two cheeseburgers, large fries and Prozac. Your arteries will still clog, but you just won't care. In fact, you'll be the happiest one in the morgue.

I hate the slogans in cheaper restaurants. Like "Have it your way." "My way" would be in a better restaurant where the tables and chair are not cemented to the floor. Unless the restaurant is located on the side of the San Andreas Fault, the tables and chairs should be movable. If I can't move, turn, breathe or burp, then it's not fine dining, it's a Scientology social.

I also hate it when restaurants lock their bathrooms and you have to get a key from the manager to get in. Why are they locked? Do their customers tend to steal the urinals when their meals are done? And what's with the gigantic key rings? The keys to the bathrooms are always attached to huge sticks or hangers that clank and make noise. Give me a normal-size key ring and I promise I'll alert all the other patrons by yelling, "I have to pish, now."

I hate the sign in the window that states: "Shirt and shoes required." Is that really necessary? Does that mean pants are optional? That as long as you have on some kind of footwear and sleeves, it's okay to have your cooz hanging out or your balls stuck to the chair? I experienced that in a restaurant one day and not only was it disgusting and unattractive and unhygienic, I also got very cold.

And finally . . . I hate vegans. God gave you incisors, so what's the problem? Not only are vegans annoying, they look sickly. Right now, fast, name twenty vegans you'd like to bang. They don't eat meat, they don't eat poultry, they don't eat fish, they don't eat anything with a face. . . . You know what? They can eat me.

THINGS NOT TO SAY AT A DINNER PARTY

- The table looks great; most of the place settings match.

- There's a pubic hair in my soup and it looks like Uncle Jack's.

- Does anyone know the difference between the early signs of chlamydia and syphilis?

- This steak is delicious! Ever been to a slaughterhouse? They kill the cow by driving a nail between its eyes.

- You'll never guess who lost a baby and left it in the toilet? No, really, c'mon, try to guess. I'll give you a hint. . . .

- Are these capers or droppings?

- Did anyone ever notice that all Down syndrome kids look alike?

- They said it was SIDS, but to perfectly honest, I never trusted the mother. . . .

- How come you never see really old midgets?

- Fuck the Jews.

- Is it just me, or does foreskin taste funny?

- Please, if I start to smell just tell me and I'll change the bag.

LOCATION. LOCATION. LOCATION . . .

. . . Are the three most important things
when you're buying a house . . .
or looking for my G-spot.

■

I have a love-hate relationship with a lot of cities and countries. As a rule, I love places that pay me to be there and I hate places that don't.

By the way, when I speak of cities I mean real cities. I don't go to "cities" where being mayor is a part-time job. Or where people brag that it's safe to leave their doors open at night. These people obviously don't have good jewelry. I don't do towns, villages, burgs, hamlets or grottos. I'm a comedian, not an elf. If Hillary Clinton wants to do a village that's her business—I just hope for her sake she finds a village where mannish women in pastel pantsuits are all the rage. The only village I love is Greenwich Village in New York City, and that's only because (a) it's not actually a village, it's a neighborhood, and (b) it's where I started my comedy career playing little clubs like Upstairs at the Downstairs and The Duplex. If it weren't for those little clubs in Greenwich Village I'd have had to pursue one of my other passions in life and instead of being the beloved star of stage and screen you are reading now, I would have become either a dental hygienist (I've always loved the thrill of a putting my hands in a strange man's mouth) or a fetish model, posing nude for magazines like *Pavement Princess*, *Gutter Gals*, and *What Do You Expect for a Quarter?*

I've gone around the world a number of times (often in the backseat of a Buick) and, having been everywhere from Bayonne to Berlin, I can say with certainty that Dorothy said it best when she said, "There's no place like home." (Meanwhile Auntie Em is thinking "Listen, bitch, we agreed to let you move back in with us after you graduated from college and couldn't find a job, but that was only supposed to be temporary. Fact is, your uncle Henry and I were going to turn your old bedroom into a sex dungeon and then maybe do a little traveling. After all, it's not like you're our real daughter, right?")

I live in New York City (except for when I live in Los Angeles with Melissa, which I'm willing to do anytime I can get a network to pay me to do it). But before I tell you all of the places that I hate, let me tell you that I love New York. (And by "New York" I mean Manhattan; anything west of Amsterdam Avenue I consider to be part of "the heartland.") Here are a few reasons why New York is the greatest city in the world:

- In New York, if someone stabs you in the head, chances are they have a very good reason to do so, i.e., you jumped in front of them on a lease application for a rent-stabilized apartment.
- New York is the fashion center of America. Even the homeless have style—and its not just knowing how to make a shopping cart into an accessory. Little do people realize the homeless have a great eye for layering. Usually I am not a fan of layering but the homeless can pull it off—a wool scarf over a bathrobe on top of a flak jacket over a pair of cargo pants with three pairs of socks but no shoes? It's a look. Again, not for me, but I'm not an autumn.
- You don't have to visit a nursing home to smell urine. Just walk down any street and the bouquet is in the air, like night-blooming jasmine with a very high acid content.
- I hate cities where people are nice. In New York you walk down the street and you hear, "Fuck you, die!!" And I love to scream right back, "Fuck you, Sister Mary Louise!"
- David Letterman is in New York. Even better— Jay Leno isn't.
- We embrace diversity: Our past five mayors were Jewish, black, tiny, gay, or had speech defects. Fabulous!
- Finally, if someone drops dead of a heart attack in Saks Fifth Avenue, the salespeople are trained to move the body out of the way so that

it doesn't impact the customer flow or purchase points.

I hate Houston. It's crawling with bugs. Oh wait, that's Whitney Houston; I'm sorry, my bad. (Can I just mention that Whitney looked fabulous at the Grammys? She was in mahogany from head to toe.)

I hate Arizona. It always eight hundred degrees outside and everybody's always saying, "But it's a dry heat!" So's the inside of my microwave. You wanna grab your bronzer and spend a couple of hours tanning? Arizona is filled with old people, asthmatics and prisoners, as well as old asthmatic prisoners. By the way, do you know what they call people in Arizona who eat dinner after 4:00 P.M.? Night owls. Arizona is the prison capital of America. Eighty percent of the population is incarcerated and the other twenty percent are on parole. In Scottsdale a prison cell is considered an efficiency apartment. The upside to Arizona is that your tax dollars go further because you don't have to buy the convicts blankets and coats or warm food.

I hate the great northwest because it's gray and rainy and depressing. The only good thing is everybody's so depressed there are thousands of suicides and that really opens up the housing market and makes it easy to buy a cheap condominium. The high suicide rates also make it easy to find parking, especially during the holidays. In Seattle there is a six-month waiting list if you want to jump off a tall building. It rains so much in Seattle the leading cause of death is mildew, followed by reading *The Bell Jar*.

I hate Savannah. It's beautiful but there's a paper mill on the river that makes the whole city smell like vomit. Spending a week in Savannah, Georgia, is like spending a weekend in Mary Kate Olsen's mouth.

I hate Florida. It's all old people, trailer parks, drug dealers and Disney World. I can handle the old people, drug dealers and trailer parks. But screaming children and a giant mouse with three fingers? Am I in Orlando or Saigon?

There are too many old people in Florida. It's like Arizona with mosquitoes. Just once I'd like to go to a dinner party where every conversation doesn't start with, "Do you remember . . . ?" followed by the name of somebody who just died. It's like the Oscars' death reel played on a continuous loop.

Floridians brag about living with crocodiles—as though building a house on stilts so you don't wind up without feet is a normal thing. Let me tell you, if I want to live with a scaly creature that has an unhinged jaw and jagged teeth I'll move in with Lea Michele.

I hate the Plains states. They're plain. There's no color, everything is wheat and grain and barley and grass. The whole region is nothing more than a Pottery

Barn with cows. The leading cause of death in Nebraska is people falling asleep. It's so dull the kids go to Kansas for their senior proms.

I hate cities that fight the elements, like Chicago, whose mottos are "It's great to be inside" and "Shut that fucking door, you idiot." Their number one export is "things that fell off the truck." Let's just hope that one good gust of wind blows Chicago into a better climate and suddenly it's Chicago, Bahamas.

I hate Austin, but it's not Austin's fault. Austin is a great city that's stuck in Texas. You can always tell when you get inside the Austin city limits because the hair is smaller and you can understand what the people are saying.

I hate New Orleans, but I respect it. You've got to respect a city that doesn't want to hear about building above sea level. Grandpa dies and he's buried over you. Even hell is up. New Orleans is filthy and dirty; it's the only city that looked better after it was hit by a category five hurricane.

Mardi Gras is fascinating—you can puke in front of all the really good hotels. In New Orleans you can wear anything and do anything and no one seems to notice; it's like hanging out at the Braille Institute.

Some people do love New Orleans—Anne Rice loves it, vampires love it; even Lee Harvey Oswald loved it and he was quite the sourpuss.

I hate San Francisco because I not only left my heart there, but my hairdresser. San Francisco is the only city in the world that has a lisp. The whole town smells like lube. It's built on hills that are so steep that when you get to the top of one of them in a taxi, you can't see what's on the other side. Going up a hill in San Francisco is like going down on Kathy Bates.

Enough with the good ol' U. S. of A. There are whole countries I hate . . .

I hate Sweden. Well, I don't actually hate Sweden, I hate *Mamma Mia* and all the acclaim Meryl Streep received for singing "Dancing Queen" slightly off-key. It's enough with Meryl, it's enough with ABBA and it's enough with all the pretty, smooth-skinned, natural blondes. Give me a couple of skanky brunettes with pockmarks and gunshot wounds and maybe, just maybe, I'll feel better about the place. Sweden is like the Plains states in that it is totally devoid of color. And I'm talking about the population, not the geography. Sweden is so white even the black people are white. It's like being at a Klan meeting with supermodels.

I hate the northern lights. Sweden is in absolute daylight six months out of the year. Who needs that? I'm not in daylight for six hours a year. My best feature is total darkness. My plastic surgeon's office is in the Howe Caverns. The northern lights are actually called the aurora borealis, and I hate that because Aurora Borealis is my porn name. I feel so violated.

The constant daylight has made the Swedes so crazy that there's a mental illness named for them: Stockholm syndrome. This is when victims of kidnap and torture begin to identify with and protect their captors instead of turning them in to the authorities. Remember when newspaper heiress Patty Hearst was kidnapped by the Symbionese Liberation Army and forced to join their radical cult? They changed her name to Tania and made her wear a beret and forced her to help rob a bank at gunpoint and people were killed, and she protected her captors and went to jail.

And as this was playing out on the news every night, one thought kept going through my head over and over: What kind of idiot wears a beret in April?

I hate cities and countries that change their names. Beijing used to be called Peking. Mumbai used to be known as Bombay. Why did they do that? Are there Google Earth lobbyists trying to make money off of new maps? This name changing thing is a huge pain in the ass; the other night I called up for Chinese food delivery and it took me almost forty-five minutes to order a large Peking duck. In the amount of time it took me to order, I could have flown to Beijing and brought the thing home myself. We don't do that name-changing crap here in America. Since day one, Los Angeles is still Los Angeles, Chicago is still Chicago. And Detroit is still a shithole.

I hate places that are incorrectly named, like Greenland, which is cold and icy. Or Iceland, which is lush and green. I think they took those names just to fuck with us.

I don't know if the Ivory Coast has any actual ivory in it, but I respect it because it's the only country named after two deodorant soaps.

I hate Paris. Yeah, yeah, yeah, it's the most beautiful city in the world, but it's inhabited by the most disgusting people. Parisians are horrible. If you ask a Parisian for help you'll die in the *rue* before they'll lend you a hand. Their yellow smiley-face buttons are smirking. Parisians always walk around with this expression on their faces like they've just smelled something rotten. Well guess what? "Hey, Jean-Claude, the smell is from you! You stink!" The French are not known for their hygiene; in fact, the level of b.o. in Paris is *tres horrible* mostly because the French always have their arms up in the air—since they're always surrendering. It is a country of smelly cowards. Do not, I repeat, *do not* stand downwind on a hot summer day on the Champs-Elysees.

I hate the pretentiousness of Parisians. They name their streets after the literati, like Rue de Victor Hugo and Rue Guy de Maupassant. The only street I like is Rue Honore de Balzac, because "Balzac" sounds so gay, and I love my gays. I might like Parisians more if they named their streets *only* for gay icons, like Rue

Liza Minnelli or Rue Bette Midler or, my favorite, Rue McClanahan.

I've always hated Maurice Chevalier. He sang "Thank Heaven for Little Girls" and the French adored him. *Creeeeepy!* In America we have a word for men like that: *Polanski*.

I've hated the French ever since Dreyfus. The affair, not the actor—although it's a crime against humanity that Richard Dreyfuss never got to do "En Paris." Be that as it may, I hate the French because they were big Nazi sympathizers. Sure, there was the so-called French "Resistance," but I put up more of fight on my wedding night. During World War II they had a rebate program, "Bring in a Jew, get a toaster." The great designer Coco Chanel was a Nazi sympathizer and a great anti-Semite. Her original fragrances were Chanel No. Fünf and Auschwitz No. Nine.

I hate Winnipeg. It's cold all the time. No matter when you go there the people are shivering and shaking. It's like being at a detox center on intake day. Winnipeg is so cold the town witch has no tits. They froze and fell off.

I hate Venice—the city in Italy, not the beach town in California. Venice, California, is just steroid-riddled bodybuilders with bulging veins and shrunken testicles. People think Venice, Italy, is canals, art and romance but actually it has more bums, drifters, vagrants and losers per square mile than anyplace else. It's like Occupy Wall Street, but everybody has better complexions because it's near the water.

If I could live my entire life no more than six blocks from Fifth Avenue I'd be perfectly happy. Okay, I wouldn't be "perfectly happy"; I'd still be sour and unpleasant, but I wouldn't mind it as much because I'd be close to shopping.

OVERRATED HISTORICAL FIGURES THAT I HATE

Hitler

First of all I hate him, hate him, hate him! Probably the worst villain of the last five hundred years and on top of that he had *zero* fashion sense. Brown shirts? Brown was over in 1839, let alone 1939. And the boots in the summer and the armbands and the guns and the epaulets—the whole look didn't work.

Hitler also had a horrible attitude. Millions of Germans would practically throw their arms out of their sockets saluting him, and he'd make this half-ass wave back at them, as if to say, "Whatever." These people are getting up early, early, early to march and sing and parade around, the women got up at the crack of dawn to iron lederhosen and put their braids on top of their heads, and all Hitler could manage in return was a faggy little wave? Nice.

George Washington

I hate him because he was stupid. In 1776, George Washington crossed the Delaware River. *February* 1776. In the winter! Across snow and ice. Who was his travel agent? Mohamed Atta? Wait till April when it thaws, big boy.

Even more shocking, he went from Pennsylvania to New Jersey? Who goes to New Jersey? Even the bridges and tunnels only charge a toll to get out.

Then there's that cherry tree nonsense. According to legend, when George was six, he took his hatchet and chopped down his father's favorite cherry tree, but he didn't get punished because he confessed to doing the dirty deed. Historians look at this episode as a study in character. I look at as a study in psychosis. What kind of six-year-old has a hatchet? And what kind of grown man has a favorite tree? And then I wonder why, even as president, he walked around in a white shoulder-length wig and tight blue capri pants.

Benjamin Franklin

I hate him because he was a total pervert. (And I know perverts: I dated two-thirds of the Osmond brothers; they're in my little black book of Mormon. And I for one can tell you why Mormons' underpants are magic.)

Benjamin Franklin discovered electricity by accident. We all know he took that stupid kite with the key on it out in the rain, but when the key got struck by lightning, he loved it. He was turned on like Michael Jackson at a Boy Scout jamboree. In fact, for the rest of his life, anytime it poured he ran out on his roof, naked, and stood there with a fork in his mouth.

Gandhi

Mo, as he liked to be called in bed, was a man on a mission, and the mission was "peace through starvation." Why he couldn't pick "peace through retail," or "peace through clever white wines," God only knows. To me, giving someone the chance to buy high-quality shoes at low discount prices is a much better marketing tool than starving to death.

Christopher Columbus

He got lost. He left Spain looking for the trade route to South America, zigged when he should have zagged, missed his turn and wound up in Rehoboth instead of Rio. In spite of his wife's pleadings, he refused to pull over and ask for directions.

Stephen Hawking

Stephen Hawking is brilliant, an absolute genius. He can drool in twelve different languages. But so what? His wife beats the shit out of him twice a week. And this is the second wife, not the first. (How he meets women at all is beyond me; the man's a coffee table with a tongue.) Stephen left the first wife for this one. I could understand it if the first one whacked him around—I mean, he did cheat on her and roll off with another woman, but why this one is turning his life into a hell on wheels is anybody's guess. But you'd think, with all of his brainpower, he'd at least have figured out how to blink 9-1-1.

Anne Frank

She only wrote the one book *and* didn't finish it. What kind of a work ethic is that? She has nothing to do all day long, yet, when it comes to completing the one task at hand, she can't be bothered. I mean c'mon, maybe this is why Peter Van Daan wasn't all that interested in hooking up. No one likes lazy.

Oprah

And don't say, "Oprah who?" You know who. Stedman's beard, that's who. Oh, please. Sure, she denies it but even Abraham Lincoln didn't have this big a beard. I know Oprah's opened schools and raised money and given away Buicks, blahblah-blahblahblah. But so what? She can't keep her weight at a reasonable level. One day she weighs 140, two days later she's being fitted for a boat cover. What kind of a role model is that? Her weight goes up and down more than Monica Lewinsky's head. And honestly, I don't know how she keeps gaining the weight; how fattening could Gayle King be?

Neil Armstrong

On July 20, 1969, Neil Armstrong walked on the moon and everyone's been carrying on about it ever since. I'm not saying it wasn't a huge accomplishment—being the first person to do anything is notable for sure. But how about a little perspective?

When Neil left Florida that morning for the moon there was no traffic. Plus, he made all the lights, so the trip itself was relatively simple. A couple of hours later he gets to the moon and lands right away. No trouble finding a parking spot. No meters, no loading zones, nothing. So he puts the parking brake on, gets out, walks around, takes a golf swing, picks up some rocks and comes home.

That's it. He didn't do any sightseeing, no shopping, no touristy stuff at all; he didn't even try to lie out and pick up a tan. He just came home. The man had the one vacation the whole fucking year; he drove eight million light-years to get to there and didn't so much as have a cup of coffee, check into a hotel or buy a T-shirt. What kind of behavior is that? That's not a hero, that's a horse's ass.

And not for nothing, he got the whole fucking vacation for free.

Paul McCartney

Paul was the "cute" Beatle, but in all honesty, that wasn't really much of a horse race, now was it? Being the cutest member of the Beatles is like being the smartest person in Sarah Palin's house—not a huge accomplishment. Compared to John, George and Ringo, *I* could be the cutest Beatle, and I can't sing or dance or play an instrument.

But it's Paul's taste in women I find so stunning. He's the richest, most famous rock star in the entire world, and he was married first to a tone-deaf mousy woman who could've been his sister, and then to Peg Leg Pete who tried to fleece him for all he was worth.

Mick Jagger looks like an extra from the Planet of the Apes and he has beautiful women hanging all over him. Billy Joel and Keith Richards? Not exactly magazine covers, yet they always have gorgeous girlfriends. Even Elton John has a pretty wife. Okay, her name is David, but still . . . you get my point.

I do feel bad for Paul that the second wife, the one-legged one, Heather Mills, turned out to be so rotten. He made her rich and famous and he even wrote special songs for her, like "I Saw Her Leaning There," "I Want to Hold Your Stump," and my favorite, "Eleanor Rigby (Leaves Her Leg in a Jar That She Keeps by the Door)." And what does she give him, in return? A kick in the ass and a trillion-dollar alimony bill, that's what.

Paul just got married again. This one's a Jewish biped. Let's hope it's third time lucky and we can all just let it be.

Jesus

Not to knock his accomplishments, but the worst carpenter ever until Richard Carpenter, who just sat at the piano smiling while his sister drummed and sang and threw up.

Everyone carries on like Jesus was the Second Coming, but let me tell you, he had flaws.

For example, in high school Jesus didn't apply himself at all. If he had, he might've gone to college, and instead of being a carpenter he might've owned a lumber company. Or at least been silent partner in a drywall business.

And did you ever see anything he built? No. In the history of the world is there one chair or bookcase or credenza that says "Built in Bethlehem"? No.

Finally: He couldn't pull himself off a cross. What kind of a carpenter can't pull himself off a cross? He didn't have a tool belt? How about carrying a hammer? Boom, boom, you pull the nails out, you clean up a little, you're at Red Lobster by eight. Eight thirty if there's desert traffic.

ROAD TRIP

In 1957, Jack Kerouac published the classic novel, *On the Road*. Twelve years later, at age forty-seven, he was dead.

Moral of the story: Stay home.

∎

I hate traveling and I think it goes all the way back to when I was a little girl. I hated traveling on horses. There I was, in my pretty little bonnet, riding through town, just me and my pa, having a perfectly nice day and all of a sudden the tail goes up on the horse in front of me. Party's over!

The only, and I mean *only*, good thing about horses is that they can poop while they walk—they are so lucky. I think about that all the time when I'm at a sale at Gucci.

I hate being on the road; quite frankly, at this point in my life I hate leaving the house altogether. If this book is a success, I may never go outside and see the light of day again. A few years from now local authorities will answer a smell complaint from my co-op board and find me, partially decomposed in a Valentino dress, under a pile of newspapers, rotting away like a housecat in an episode of *Hoarders*. And all of my neighbors will say, "Who knew Joan was such a homebody?"

I've been on the road for my entire life. I remember the day I told my father that I wanted to be a comedian; he was so wonderful and supportive. We were sitting in the living room and he put his hands on my shoulders, looked me in the eye and said, "Joan, get the fuck out." Since then it's been hotels and motels and inns and condos and planes and trains and buses and camels. (I once played a Giggle Factory in Cairo. Talk about kill or be killed.)

Life on the road is not as glamorous as you would think. Oh sure, there's the occasional chiropodist from Ohio who can help turn a Red Roof Inn into a Bunny Ranch, but otherwise life on the road is hell. Remember when Willie Nelson sang, "On the Road Again"? Did you know the record company made him change the original lyrics? What Willie actually wrote was, "On the road, again, oh Christ I can't believe I'm on the road again." Even he hated it and he was stoned all the time.

I hate flying. Flying used to be so much fun. I remember the first flight I ever took; I was about sixteen and I got on the plane and said to the pilot, "Orville, I hope you and Wilbur make this a smooth flight." And he said, "Fuck off, prissy bitch." Ahh, memories.

> Did you know that the slogan "Something special in the air" was about American Airlines? I always thought it was about Ricky Martin's ass.

I hate stewardesses who insist on being called *flight attendants.* It's soooo pretentious, what's the point? You're doing the exact same job as before so what does it matter what I call you? The same woman has been working as my proctologist's assistant for twenty years. She's always been known as a proctologist's assistant. Not once in all that time has she ever said to me, "Joan, from now on I insist on being referred to as a doody handler." What was wrong with "stewardess," anyway? It's the female version of "steward." I hate women who say, "steward*ess* is pejorative. It implies we're less than men." You know who I've never heard make that complaint? Count*esses.* They seem just fine with it. I say, as long as the castle, the land, the servants and the jewels are in my name, you can call me Cuntess for all I care.

I hate preflight announcements. The first thing flight attendants say is that their main priority is safety. "Hi, I'm Missy from your Minneapolis-based flight crew and before we push back from the gate, please remember, our primary purpose is to keep you safe." Wrong!!! Your primary purpose is to keep me happy. The pilot will keep me safe. Your first responsibility is to tell those whiny brats in row seven to stop kicking and shut the fuck up or I'm going to call Casey Anthony. Your secondary purpose is fresh-brewed decaf and third on your priority list is making sure that the in-flight movie isn't *Alive*. "Safety" is not really part of your job. Sorry, Missy, but I just don't think you and your perkiness are going to be much help in a plunging jumbo jet.

I hate when flight attendants try to be funny with their announcements. Until you can do forty-five minutes on a Friday for three thousand drunken carpet salesmen in Vegas, leave the comedy to me. I won't try to explain how to exit a burning fuselage and you don't try to make the Asian high rollers laugh by walking down the aisle and saying, "Hey, srant-eyes, where you flom?"

> **United Airlines used to have friendly skies. "Friendly skies" meant that the female flight attendants would give blow jobs in the galley. Things have changed. Now only the male flight attendants give blow jobs in the galley.**

I hate *old* flight attendants. They can be very cranky and sour. You enter the plane from the Jetway and there to greet you is Nettie from Kitty Hawk. She has so many "years of service" wings pinned to her blouse her boobs could take off by themselves.

Old flight attendants break down. Oxygen masks drop down every fifteen minutes—for her, so she has the strength to get from business class all the way to coach. She comes down the aisle with her cart, which in her case is really just a walker with snacks, and says, "Coffee, tea . . . Maalox?" I asked her, "What time do we land?" She replied, "Daddy likes soup." My opinion? If you trained with Icarus you shouldn't still be serving coffee in coach.

I hate it when my flight arrives early and there is no gate available at the airport. It completely defeats the idea of being early. "Good news from the cockpit, ladies and gentlemen: We're going to arrive forty minutes ahead of schedule. Unfortunately there's no gate available so we're going to be sitting on the tarmac until mid-October." Why is there no gate available? Did the airline not know we were coming? Did we just drop out of the sky and surprise them? When a baby is born prematurely does the doctor come in and say, "Good news, the baby is fine. Unfortunately we don't have any incubators available so we're going to leave her in the lobby near the soda machine for a while"?

I hate airlines that make you pay extra for everything. (Which is pretty much all of them except for Southwest. On Southwest the amenities are free but you have to pay for their pilots' rehab stints at Betty Ford.)

Some airlines charge six bucks for a blanket. And they're not even blankets; they're bibs that got out of hand. They're barely big enough to keep one tiny part of your body a little bit warm, maybe your hands or your feet or, if you're Asian, your junk.

I hate paying baggage fees. Paying an airline extra to carry your baggage is insane. It's like to going to a restaurant and having to pay extra for the plates. If you say "no" what are they going to do, dump piles of food in your lap? The airlines should be thrilled we have luggage, because you know who travels with no luggage? Terrorists and shoe bombers, that's who. If I have luggage with me you know you're safe—no way am I going to blow up a five thousand dollar Louis Vuitton ValPak.

> **Delta Air Line's slogan was, "Delta is ready when you are." Really? Then have the plane pick me up at 6:00, I'll be in my driveway. I'll be the one in the red jacket with the suitcase.**

I hate what now passes for food and snacks on planes. What's with the blue potato chips? The only things on the plane that should be blue are the uniforms, the pilot's balls and the veins on the old flight attendant's legs. In the old days they'd put a tablecloth on your tray and you'd have your choice of steak or chicken or fish. It was like a bar mitzvah without the complaining. Now they *sell* you boxes of crackers and slices of apples that looked like they were picked in the Garden of Eden.

The only thing I hate more than some morbidly obese slob waddling down the aisle looking for his seat is trying to look busy so I don't have to make eye contact with him while praying that the seat he's looking for isn't next to mine—and if it is, I encourage him to rethink sitting there by saying something like, "Do you know how to change a colostomy bag?"

I hate flying with Alec Baldwin. He's a good actor and a funny man, but honestly, unless the electronic device you're fiddling around with is a pacemaker or a porn app, then turn the fucking thing off. Scrabble can wait until you land.

I hate people who whine about airport security. Not only does the added security not bother me, I actually like it. And not because it makes me feel safe, but because it makes me feel moist. I can't wait for the TSA agents at the airport to pat me down. It's like sex without the apologies. I can't get patted down often enough. I'm at the age where they're the only ones who want to touch me and that's only because they have to. You know how most people take off their shoes when going through the scanner? I take off my dress. I'm at the point where I demand a cavity search just to get on a crosstown bus.

My favorite part of the screening process is being wanded, when the TSA agent starts rubbing that electronic magic wand all over me. It gets me all hot and bothered. In fact, when the agent is finished wanding me I sit on the baggage carousel, have a cigarette and sing "The Man That Got Away."

Sometimes I actually hide contraband in my Spanx just to get patted down. There's a tall, dark and handsome TSA agent at JFK who had to pat me down six times. He and I still correspond.

But you know what else I hate? Those new X-ray scanning machines that let the agents see right through your clothes. First off, they're used in lieu of the pat downs and wandings. I hate that. (I also hate the term "in lieu of.") Second, the agents can see everything: moles, scars, implants—it's not right! I shouldn't have to coif my muff just to walk through an X-ray machine.

I hate people who sneak into first class to use the bathroom. I'm sitting there, in 4F, sipping Cristal and admiring my new line of jewelry for QVC, and suddenly, busting through the curtain and rushing toward the bathroom is some doughy soccer mom holding her crotch and yelling, "Emergency, emergency!" No, it's not!!! Opening the main hatch and pushing you out at thirty thousand feet for disturbing me is an emergency. Peeing on your brown stretch pants is really just a problem; and it's your problem, not mine. I know that in first class there are four passengers and eleven bathrooms and in coach there are a thousand passengers and only one half bath and a broken chamber pot, but I'm in first class for a reason, and the reason is *because* I don't want to pee with you. I say, "Get back in your cabin, grab a couple of paper towels, and look at the bright side: You're wearing polyester, it doesn't hold a stain."

I hate flying on private jets. When someone takes me on a private jet I'm always treated like a queen, but because I'm a guest it means that whoever owns the jet is a lot more rich and famous than I am and if that private jet goes down, the obituary in the *New York Times* will read: INTERNATIONAL OIL MAGNATE SHEIK ABDULLAH MUCKETY MUCK AND FOUR OTHER (POORER) PEOPLE DIE IN PRIVATE PLANE CRASH. I haven't spent forty years playing one-nighters in Wilkes-Barre to die as an "other." So keep your private fucking planes. I'm more than happy to keep badgering commercial airlines into upgrading me to first class.

It's not just planes I hate. I hate all forms of public transportation. "Why?" you ask. "What's wrong with public transportation?" And I always answer, "The public, that's what."

People are pigs. Not all people—not you, for example. You bought this book, so even if you threw the bag and the receipt on the sidewalk I'd overlook your pig-gishness because I have your money. But other people are pigs—especially bus people.

I hate bus people. There are only a few kinds of people who truly like to travel by bus: country music stars, white trash, single mothers who were thrown out of their motel rooms for leaving cigarette burns on the night tables and dangerous felons just released from prison. Oh, and old ladies with buckets of nickels on their way to Atlantic City to piss away their Medicare money.

I hate Greyhound's motto: "Leave the driving to us." It's so stupid. What do they think—that I'm planning to take a shift behind the wheel? Suddenly I'm going to vault from my seat, hurdle down the aisle, push the driver out of the way and steer the big rig on its coveted Akron-to-Sheboygan run? Look, I'm only traveling by bus because I have an infectious cough that prohibits me from traveling by plane and spreading germs to people who have more money, power and influence than you do.

I hate it when the local bus has to stop to let a handicapped person on. What a friggin' nuisance. Everyone else has to wait while the driver stops the bus, lowers the ramp down, loads the paraplegic, locks him into place, raises the ramp, and then starts the bus back up. It makes no sense. I'm late for a pedicure appointment and have to wait for someone who can't even feel his toes? That's just plain wrong.

I hate that the first few rows on city buses are reserved for the elderly. I'm tired of tripping over their canes, walkers and companion animals.

Where could they have to go in such a rush that they have to sit right up front near the door—a Widows Without Partners Dance-a-Thon? A new job as a phone sex operator? (I knew a ninety-three-year-old woman who supplemented her Social Security by working on a sex hotline. She was so senile she'd answer the phone and say, "What am *I* wearing?" The heavy breathing was easy for her; she had emphysema.)

I hate following a man into the toilet on a bus. (When I say "following him" I don't mean chasing him down the aisle for a quickie; I mean going in there to do my business after he's finished doing his.) How can I put this delicately—men seem to think that the bowl is merely a suggestion. Also, please note—how a man goes to the bathroom on a bus tells you what kind of a lover he is. If a man can't hit a hole the size of three basketballs in a fully lit john, how's he going to perform in a dark room?

I hate country stars who like traveling in giant customized buses so they can schlep their entire families with them: parents, kids, grandkids, goats . . . Look, I appreciate the sentiment; family is an important thing, but . . . Dolly, Willie, Garth . . . I know your hearts are in the right place, but seriously, you're spending millions of dollars on a bus? When Melissa was a child and I was on the road I took her everywhere I went. But never once did I think about buying her a bus; until she was twelve, she fit perfectly into the overhead. When she got a little older I sent her via cargo—I was told it was usually heated, and she wasn't in the same compartment as the luggage.

I hate the New York City subway system. They're not train cars, they're urinals with wheels. And they're dangerous. If I want to spend time locked up with a creepy, stinky old perv, I'll pay a conjugal visit to Phil Spector.

I hate boats. I hate traveling on any form of transportation that can be overtaken by pirates. It's 2012—how is it there are still pirates? Shouldn't they be extinct by now? After all, we've managed to phase out pilgrims, cavemen and folk singers; surely we can do something about Smee, Blackbeard and Captain Hook. I'm not an expert on maritime law but can't we call the Spanish Armada to come in and get rid of them? Unless the pirates look like Johnny Depp (in his younger days, not his present "I live in France so now I look filthy" stage), in which case they can kidnap and ravage me as often as their schedules allow.

I hate cruising. At sea. However, cruising a nursing home for a ninety-year-old man with ninety million in the bank is a whole 'nother story.

The only time people think about ships is when there's a blurb on the news about a ship that either sank or someone fell or was pushed overboard, or it's taken hostage by foreign enemies. If you think I'm kidding try to name five ships that are famous for something other than sinking. Go ahead, I'll wait. Time's up; I rest my case.

The *only* hit movies about ships were about ships that sank: *Titanic, The Poseidon Adventure*, and *PT-109*, the story of JFK going down at sea instead of on Marilyn Monroe.

And by the way, did you know that referring to a ship as a "boat" is considered bad luck, like whistling in a dressing room, or stepping on a crack?* According to sailors, boats sink and ships don't. Really? Then apparently the *Titanic* was just a boat. And by the way, the *Titanic* didn't sink because it hit an iceberg; it sank because Kate Winslet was fat. If someone had put that British hag on Weight Watchers, Leonardo DiCaprio would never have drowned in the Atlantic.

I know what you're thinking: *But* The Love Boat *didn't sink*. Stop whining! For starters *The Love Boat* was

---

*FYI: I never bought the "step on a crack, break your mother's back" thing. The only way that works is if mommie dearest is already lying facedown on the sidewalk from your initial rabbit punch to the back of her head, and then you step on the crack.

a TV show, not a movie. It's where has-beens went for one last shot at keeping their Screen Actors Guild cards before they died. Sort of like *Celebrity Appren* . . . Never mind, bad analogy.

I hate cruises—especially three-day cruises. Even Leon Klinghoffer was on the goddamned ship for a couple of Tuesdays. Where can you go in three days? The first day you're still in Staten Island, then you go to the Jersey Shore, and then you have to turn around and go back. That's not a cruise, that's a ferry without a GPS. Three days doesn't make it for me. If I go on a cruise it's got to be at least a week and the "exotic" ports of call can't be in Maryland or Virginia.

I hate "the captain's table." Being invited to have dinner at the captain's table is supposed to be some kind of an honor, but I never understood why. What if the captain is dull or stammers or eats with his elbows on the table? Then it's not an honor, it's a sentence. When I take a plane to Europe I don't have dinner on the pilot's lap. When I go downtown in a taxi I don't have brunch at the driver's mosque.

Is the captain such a good host? Is he the Martha Stewart of the high seas? To me an honor is winning an Academy Award or having Judge Judy give you a huge settlement in a questionable malpractice suit you filed. But dinner with a sailor? Please, Popeye was a sailor. Spinach for two is not exactly my idea of haute cuisine.

You have to be invited to sit at the captain's table, you can't just plunk your ass down and say, "Hey, Skipper, how's it hangin'?" These invites are hard to come by. It's easier to get an audience with the pope than to get an invitation to the captain's table. And I'd rather sit with the pope—his drag is *faaaaabulous*.

Cruise ships have morgues on board in case one of the passengers goes "anchors aweigh." If you're going to have a morgue on board, placement is important. Don't put the morgue next to the dining room; not only is having the first seating next to The Last Supper déclassé, it also makes you wonder what the meat is for dinner. Having a morgue on board is just creepy. You could be at the midnight buffet looking at the beautiful seafood spread and suddenly realize that the ice chips surrounding your shrimp cocktail at twelve o'clock might have been surrounding Mrs. Blickstein's body at eleven.

I hate gay cruises. They're too gay, even for me, and I love love love my gays. Gay cruises are all about hundreds of gay men drinking, carrying on and having sex. Or, hundreds of gay women drinking and carrying on and building bookcases.

I hate whale watching. It's stupid. You spend hundreds of dollars to stand on a boat, getting soaked and nauseous just to watch a whale jump around. Save your money—stay home and throw in a DVD of *Precious*.

I hate rich celebrities who lounge around naked on their private yachts. The paparazzi have long-range lenses, so keep your privates private! Unless you're Brad and Angelina, I don't want to get to know you up close and personal. Years ago in *Hustler* magazine Larry Flynt printed nude photos of Jacqueline Kennedy taken on Ari Onassis's yacht. I was shocked! Jackie had quite the muff; talk about a grassy knoll.

Traveling in foreign lands is annoying. I hate rickshaws. They're just pedicabs with peasants. If I'm in a rush, exactly how fast is a ninety-year-old woman with tightly bound feet and a hunchback going to get me to my appointed destination?

I hate traveling by camel. They are not air-conditioned and they smell worse than the New York City subway. Riding on a camel may be the only circumstance under which getting humped is actually not fun.

MY FAVORITE FIRST LADIES

When Lady Bird Johnson died, I was heartbroken. All I could think was, *First Eleanor, then Bess, then Mamie, now this. Where have all the pretty girls gone?*

Here is my short list of my favorite first ladies:

Nancy Reagan
She's the premier charter member of the First Ladies' Hall of Fame. No matter what was going on in the world, she was always able to properly accessorize red. That's a hero.

Betty Ford
She drank, she smoked, she had things removed; you could talk to her.

Martha Washington
Hot. George had wooden teeth. Martha had splinters in her thighs. 'Nuff said.

Dolly Madison
If not for her we'd all be having sorbet for dessert.

Helen Taft
William Howard Taft weighed six thousand pounds. That Helen could *schtup* him and still have the strength to smile for the cameras in the rose garden . . . a miracle worker.

Jackie Kennedy

JFK not only diddled Judith Exner, but also Marilyn Monroe, Angie Dickinson, Jayne Mansfield . . . every actress he could find. He probably banged Lassie. He slept with more famous women than Rosie O'Donnell. And Jackie knew it and didn't care. She just kept cashing the checks. I ran into her once and not only was she nice but she looked stunning. I said to her, "My God, that pink suit is fantastic on you." And she said, "Thanks. Would you believe I just got it back from the cleaners? Good as new. Madame Paulette. She's a little expensive but well worth it; believe it or not, this was covered with blood and bits of brain."

What could I say? She shared her dry cleaner's name with me. The woman was a giver.

Eleanor Roosevelt

You know that old expression, "Looks don't matter?" Eleanor took it to heart, and made homely women everywhere feel better about themselves. Eleanor was way ahead of her time. If she were alive today she'd have her own series on Animal Planet.

Abraham Lincoln

There was talk.

THE NAME GAME

A rose by any other name would smell just as sweet.

—THE BARD OF STRATFORD-UPON-AVON

A rose by any other name would be a different fucking flower, asshole.

—THE BITCH FROM *FASHION POLICE*

■

I hate nicknames. They're stupid, confusing and a complete waste of time. (Not that I have anything better to do, I just enjoy complaining.) Nicknames are usually a shorter version of a formal name or a term of endearment, but not always. Sometimes nicknames don't make sense. I hate that. For example, the nickname for Margaret is Peggy. Where does that come from? How is the nickname for William "Billy"? Where did the *B* come from? The nickname for William should be *Willy*—that makes perfect sense. And honestly, other than Rosie O'Donnell, who doesn't like a good willy? I see why a person named Jeffrey would be called *Jeff*, or Edward would be called *Eddie*, or Elizabeth would be called *Liz*. But that doesn't explain why my aunt Eleanor was called Cuntface.

Nicknames are nothing new. They've been around since the beginning of time. Little known fact: Jesus' good friends—the ones that really knew him—always called him "Jimbo."

Remember Vlad the Impaler? Everyone thinks he was nicknamed the Impaler because he killed people by running spears through them. Not so. He was called the Impaler because he was married to Myra, the Distended Vagina.

How about Ivan the Terrible? Why was he called "the terrible"? There are three reasons: one, he killed a million serfs; two, he was constantly interrupting his mother; and three, he liked to fart in closed spaces. Did you know that Ivan the Terrible had a stepbrother, Seth the Mildly Irritating?

Alexander the Great? He was named this by his Jewish mother, Miriam, who played favorites. Truth be told, Alexander was only great compared to his brother, Vinny, the Total Disappointment, who instead of going to medical school worked in a Korean deli.

I hate that states have nicknames and I hate even more that they're lies. For example, New Jersey is nicknamed "The Garden State." Really? Have you ever smelled New Jersey? Secaucus smells like a slaughterhouse; Elizabeth smells like an oil refinery and the shore smells like JWoww.

Utah is called "The Beehive State." Is that because the women there still dress like it's 1962 or because they live like bees—all sleeping on top of each other in a place everyone else is afraid to enter?

Florida is called "The Sunshine State." What a misnomer. When is the last time you saw a cheerful, smiley person in Florida? The old Jews are always complaining, the rednecks have no teeth and the immigrants are in hiding. The only person in Florida who's even a tad sunny is David Caruso, and that's because he films his show in California.

Arkansas is "The Natural State." By "natural" do they mean the women don't wax and the men sleep with their kinfolk?

Wyoming has two nicknames and they're both wrong: "The Equality State" and "The Cowboy State." Unless there are millions of cowboys and they're all the exact same size, I say, "Liar, liar, pants on fire." For the sake of accuracy, Wyoming should be called "The Local-Boy Dick Cheney Likes to Shoot His Friends in the Face State."

I could go on forever . . . and I will, in the States of the Union, a little later on.

I hate parochial schools with names. I grew up in New York. Our schools didn't have names, they had numbers, like P.S. 68 . . . or for the slutty kids, P.S. 69. But the Catholic school in my neighborhood was called Our Lady of Perpetual Motion. It was the only school that gave scholarships for St. Vitus's Dance.

There were other Catholic schools with names like Jesus the Savior or Christ the King. This upset me as I never saw a Jewish school named Elliott the Gonif or Schmuel the Inseam Specialist or Murray the Furrier. (I imagine they'd have a fascinating football team; the quarterback would start calling signals, "Thirty-two, thirty-three, thirty-three and a half, thirty-three extra long . . . Lenny, do we have this with cuffs and a pleat?")

I hate people who give themselves grandiose nicknames. Frank Sinatra was known as the "Chairman of the Board" and "Ol' Blue Eyes." I think it was selfish, selfish, selfish of him to have two nicknames. Apparently he was not only a crooner but a hoarder, too. One nickname would have been enough. Frank should have stuck with "Chairman of the Board" and let Sammy Davis, Jr., and Sandy Duncan share "Ol' Blue Eyes."

Michael Jackson was called the "King of Pop" and Benny Goodman was called the "King of Swing" and Johnny Carson was called the "King of Late Night." I think if you want be a king then you have to kneel down in front of a queen. Just like Carson Kressley does. Only Carson isn't really a king and the queen he's kneeling in front of isn't Elizabeth, it's Stanley.

And can I just say that the only king I actually knew was Marvin, "The Zipper King of Flushing," and he didn't have a career in showbiz, he had a showroom.

I hate celebrities who change their names "for show business." That's the most ridiculous thing in the world to do, or my name's not Joan Molinsky Rosenberg.

In the old days, Hollywood was run by studios and the bosses owned the stars, and they would change their names to protect their investments. And in a way, I understand. Cary Grant's real name was Archie Leach. "Cary Grant" sounds like a movie star. "Archie Leach" sounds like a primitive medical treatment. The great dancer Cyd Charisse was born Tula Finklea. I wouldn't talk to anyone named Tula, let alone let them touch my Finklea. And I don't understand why, if she was going to change her name from "Tula," she would change it to "Cyd." I hate names that aren't gender specific, like "Jamie" or "Pat" or "Kelly." "Cyd" doesn't sound like the name of a gorgeous woman with million-dollar legs; it sounds like the name of a fifty-eight-year-old discount haberdasher from Weehawken, New Jersey.

Everyone knows that Marilyn Monroe's real name was Norma Jean Baker, but did you know that John Wayne's real name was Marion Morrison? Butch, huh? Sounds less like a cowboy than a librarian with a yeast infection.

Tony Curtis was born Bernie Schwartz, but the Hollywood muckety-mucks, i.e., the self-loathing Jews who ran the studios, thought it sounded too Jewish so they changed it to Tony Curtis. I don't know if they were right or not, but the man became a huge star. Ditto with Kirk Douglas, who was born Issur Danielovitch. Kirk was feisty, though. I hear that when they asked him to change his name because it was too Jewish he wanted to change it to Kirk Lookatmybeautifulcircumcisedpenis.

And yet when Caryn Johnson becomes "Whoopi Goldberg" it isn't too Jewish; times have changed.

A lot of rappers change their names, frequently to beverage items. Ice-T was born Tracy Marrow; Ice Cube was O'Shea Jackson; and Vanilla Ice was Robert Van Winkle. Should I ever become a rapper I would change my name to "I Asked for No Ice in My Soda."

I hate Paris Hilton. Not because she has no talent or because she's a big skank ho, but because she's named after the city of Paris. And I hate the city of Paris, which I already explained to you, in another chapter, *mes amis*. But it's not just Paris Hilton that annoys me. I hate Savannah, Brooklyn, Austin, and Dallas, too. When Hillary Clinton said, "It takes a village," she didn't mean you should name your children Levittown and Kalamazoo. She meant we should collectively, as one, beat the shit out of parents who name their children Pacoima or Secaucus. If you're going to name your kids after towns and villages then be original—"This is my son, Little Rock, and my daughter, Bangor. And I believe you know the twins, Perth and Amboy? And their bull dyke cousin, Buffalo?"

I hate babies with trendy names like Tiffany and Britney and Heather and Noah and Blake and Justin. I'm sick of Olivia and Chloe and Eva and Madison. I hope Aiden and Jayden and Braden and Graden all suffer minor head injuries while reading Dr. Seuss. Enough already with the cutesy-poo baby names. What happened to *John* and *Dave* and *Sue*? Babies with trendy names grow up to be adults with ridiculous names.

"This is our CEO, Micah." "You know what, *Micah*? I want my money back. I'm closing my portfolio. I'm going with Mic*hael*. He's a grown-up."

One day all of these trendy-named children will grow up and become parents and then grandparents, and it's all wrong. Grandma Tori? Zayda Jared? Nana Savannah?

A lot of people think that all maniacs and murderers have three names. I hate that. That's soooo cliché. Yes, *some* madmen do have three names—John Wayne Gacy, Lee Harvey Oswald, Mark David Chapman—but not all. For example, Adolf Hitler didn't go by Adolf Terri Hitler. It wasn't Saddam Todd Hussein. And nobody refers to Mahmoud Bobby Ahmadinejad. There are *puh*-lenty of nut jobs who only use two names, like Charles Manson, Ted Bundy, Jeffrey Dahmer and Hannibal Lecter. These psychos had self-respect; they didn't need three names to make their point. They were men! "We're crazy and we're proud!"

I hate black people that give their children preposterous names. "Refrigerator" is not a name, it's an appliance. Lashonda, Latiqua, Lakisha, Laquandra, Latrine, Lamode and Labia are not names; they're jumble puzzles from the *Daily News*. And there are other people who don't think those names are ethnocentric; they think they're stupid. Don't take my word for it: Ask Condoleezza Rice. I'll bet even she thinks they're bullshit.

I hate that black people can't decide what they want to be called. First they were "colored," then "Negro," then "black." After that they became "people of color" and now they're "African-American." I say: Pick one! White people aren't that smart; we can't follow. I'll call you ultrasuperduperstar if it makes you happy, but for God's sake give me a final answer! The back-and-forth is giving me a migraine. And, can I just say that I don't understand ethnocentricity? For example, where did "African-American" come from? My friend Beverly always says, "I'm African-American." And I always say, "You're from Massapequa Park. Exactly where in Africa is that? Is it part of the Serengeti or maybe Kenya adjacent?" Last time I checked Massapequa Park was four stops after Bellmore on the Long Island Railroad.

Italian-Americans, Irish-Americans, Polish-Americans, etc., only refer to themselves like that when they want a big parade in their honor, so they can drink in public and get alternate side of the street parking waived. Otherwise they're plain old Americans.

And FYI, no one has ever, in my 239 years on this planet, called me a Hebraic-American. Jew bitch? All the time, but Hebraic-American bitch? Never.

I hate people who name their children as though they're still living in the "old country." The children and grandchildren of Holocaust survivors are big on this. I assume it's the result of that "never again" mentality because surely they can remember the camps without naming their kids like it's 1939 Warsaw. I don't want to go to my grandson's school play and discover that Dorothy and the Wicked Witch are being played by Chava and Ruchel.

I hate Chinese names because I can't figure out which is the first name and which is the last name, and quite frankly, neither can the Chinese. Is it Dong Ding Ding or Ding Dong Ding or Ding Ding Dong . . . or are they all really just Avon ladies? I'm afraid to get Chinese names wrong because they're a very proud people and instead of calling someone by their name I might accidentally be ordering sub gum duck. (And by "proud" I mean inherently angry and frequently armed with small explosives.)

I hate that there are 800 trillion people in Russia and they only have seven names to work with. Alexi, Sergei, Vladimir, Nicolai, Boris, Viktor and Mikhail. If you think I'm wrong try and name thirty Russians who are not named that. Yes, yes, every now and then you'll find a Leonid or Ruslan, but those are novelty names; they're the Lashonda and Laquisha of Russia. And by the way, I say "Russia," not "the former Soviet Union." Who am I, Tom fucking Brokaw?

I hate that we can name dogs based on their appearance but we can't do the same with people. A lot of dogs are named for their physical characteristics. My friend has a chocolate Lab named Cocoa. Another friend has a white Samoyed named Snowball. My neighbor has a Dalmatian named Spot. And the guy across the street has a hairless Chihuahua named Marc Anthony.

I think people should be named the same way we name our dogs. It would make life a lot simpler. Let's say you're at Sotheby's for an auction (I was there for the Elizabeth Taylor jewelry sale. Screw the Krupp Diamond, I was in awe of the pearl earrings shaped like gravy boats), and you run into a guy you know you've met before but you can't remember who the fuck he is. If you're with friends, you can work out a system where they cover you by introducing themselves so you don't have to stall while you're trying to remember his name so you don't look like a schmuck. That's an awful lot of work just to be gracious to someone you don't give a shit about. However, if his parents had the decency to name him the same way they named their pets *you* wouldn't be in an awkward position, and instead of having that uncomfortable "Geez, I think I met him in Cleveland and his name might be Frank" moment, you'd be able to walk up and say, "Hello, Lazy Eye, it's so nice to see you again!"

If we can say, "These are my dogs, Fluffy, Curly, Brownie and Whitey," then shouldn't we be able to say, "These are my children, Backfat, Lardass, Pockmarks and Clubfoot"?

I love gangster nicknames. And I say that because if I say I hate them I'm afraid I'll wind up in the trunk of a Buick and I'll have spent thirty million dollars on Botox for nothing.

I remember turning on the TV and hearing about "Lucky" Luciano, and I thought, *The man spent thirty years in prison, was shot in the face and had a droopy eye . . . What kind of luck is that?* And then there was George "Pretty Boy" Floyd, who compared to Al Capone was pretty, but compared to Brad Pitt was an absolute dog. Also back in the day there was Al Capone, who was called "Scarface," which is ironic, because today that's what we call Jocelyn Wildenstein.

In the beginning John Gotti was known as the "Teflon Don," because no crimes he committed ever stuck to him, but then he went to jail for life. I wonder if he then became known as "The Guy Who Forgot to Use Pam?"

My favorite was the famous Jewish mobster, Israel Alderman, who was called "Ice Pick Willie." He could murder someone *and* help with catering at the same time. Perfect.

STATES OF THE UNION

New York is called "The Empire State" because of its wealth and diversity. I always thought it was named for Empire Szechuan on Columbus Avenue, but what do I know? Anyway, there are a lot better nicknames for New York than "The Empire State." In fact, there are better, more thoughtful names for every state than the ones they actually have. . . .

Alabama: The Yellowhammer State

Should be called

> The Room Temperature I.Q. State
>
> *or*
>
> The Dull-Normal State
>
> *or*
>
> The Everybody Has Grandpa's Eyes State

Alaska: The Last Frontier

Should be called

> The July 11th and The Rest Is Winter State
>
> *Or*
>
> The Let's Gun Down Dinner State
>
> *Or*
>
> The Elk Don't Have a Fuckin' Chance State

Arizona: The Grand Canyon State

Should be called

The Early-Bird Special State

or

The Get Your Kids Off My Lawn State

or

The Let's Lock Up Mexicans State

or

The Land of Old Asthmatics State

Arkansas: The Natural State

Should be called

The Airborne Virus State

or

The Hillary's Considered Pretty Here State

or

The Mouth-Breathers State

California: The Golden State

Should be called

The Governor Diddled the Cleaning Lady State

or

The State That's Pulled So Tight San Diego Is Now North of Los Angeles State

Colorado: The Centennial State

Should be called

The Lots and Lots of White People State

or

The Altitude Is Better Than Crack State

or

The John Denver Loved Us but Who Gives a Fuck Now That He's Dead State

Connecticut: The Constitution State

Should be called

The Gateway to More Interesting States

or

The Would You Like Butter on Your Pastrami Sandwich? State

Delaware: The First State

Should be called

The There's Nothing Here So Leave Us Alone State

or

The Desperately in Need of a Makeover State

Florida: The Sunshine State

Should be called

The I Have a Coupon State

or

The White Trash and *Altacocker* State

or

The Shaped Like an Uncut Penis State

or

Land of a Million AARP Members

Georgia: The Peach State

Should be called

The We Miss Slavery State

or

The If You Think We're Stupid, Try Alabama State

or

The Home of the 3 Rs: Readin', 'Ritin and Racism

Hawaii: The Aloha State

Should be called

The Kenya of the Pacific

or

The It's Prettier on Postcards State

or

The Welcome Lepers, We're Willing to Chance It State

Idaho: The Gem State

Should be called

The Even Iowa Makes Fun of Us State

or

The Other White Supremacist State

or

The If We're the Gem State, Why Is the Bedazzler So Popular Here? State

Illinois: The Prairie State

Should be called

The Lincoln Was Definitely a Homo State
or
The Prairie Life Sucks State
or
The Chicago and Not Much Else State

Indiana: The Hoosier State

Should be called

The Even We Don't Know What a Hoosier Is State
or
The Indy 500 and 364 Days of Boring State

Iowa: The Hawkeye State

Should be called

The Drive Through Us Sometime State
or
The Now with Three Black People State
or
The Even Buddhists Are Bored Shitless State

Kansas: The Sunflower State

Should be called

> The Attention Homos: Dorothy's from Here State
>
> *or*
>
> The Wizard of Blahs State
>
> *or*
>
> The We Haven't Had a Good Mass Murder Since the Clutter Family in '59 State

Kentucky: The Bluegrass State

Should be called

> A Yawner After the Kentucky Derby State
>
> *or*
>
> The It's OK to Whip a Darkie on the Porch State
>
> *or*
>
> The It's Not Bluegrass, You're Just Really High State

Louisiana: The Pelican State

Should be called

> The State That FEMA Forgot
>
> *or*
>
> The Land of Floating Poor People
>
> *or*
>
> The Tryin' to Pass Off Cajun and Creole as English State
>
> *or*
>
> The Enough with Jazz, Learn a Fucking Melody Already State

Maine: The Pine Tree State

Should be called

> The Nova Scotia with Dockers State
>
> *or*
>
> The So Creepy Even Stephen King Gets Scared State
>
> *or*
>
> The More Old Lesbians Than Wisconsin State

Maryland: The Old Line State

Should be called

> The Guess Why They're Called Balti*moron*s State
>
> *or*
>
> The, Except for Courtney Love, Best Place to Catch Crabs State
>
> *or*
>
> The Francis Scott Key Wrote the National Anthem Here as Well as Its Little Known B-Side, "Baby Got Back" State

Massachusetts: The Bay State

Should be called

> The Birthplace of Freedom and a Million Kennedys State
>
> *or*
>
> The Nobody Understands Our Fucking Accent State
>
> *or*
>
> The Paul Revere Yelled, "The British Are Coming" and Then Went to P-Town and Added "In My Mouth" State

Michigan: The Great Lakes State

Should be called

The Who *Isn't* Unemployed? State

or

The Always Whining About Something State

or

The It Was Even Too Skanky for Madonna State

Minnesota: The North Star State

Should be called

The Land of 10,000 Lakes and 100,000 Hunting
Accidents

or

The Cold as a Motherfucker State

or

Minnesota: The Much Better on Paper State

Mississippi: The Magnolia State

Should be called

The Stereotype Is *Totally* True State

or

The We Is Not Dumb State

or

The State That Got Held Back a Year

or

The Land of 500 Teeth

Missouri: The Show Me State

Should be called

> The I Showed It to You—and My Case Comes Up Tuesday—State
>
> *or*
>
> The Keeping Kansas from Seeping into the Smarter States State
>
> *or*
>
> The It's Still 1953 State

Montana: The Treasure State

Should be called

> The Now with Basic Cable! State
>
> *or*
>
> The Almost Fully Lit State
>
> *or*
>
> The What's the Point, Really? State

Nebraska: The Cornhusker State

Should be called

> The Cheap, Unskilled Labor State
>
> *or*
>
> The Flatter Than Kate Moss's Chest State
>
> *or*
>
> The Barely Worth Two Choices in this Chapter State

Nevada: The Silver State

Should be called

The Slots and Sluts State

or

The Land of the Losers

or

The Roy Got Eaten by a Tiger but Siegfried's Still Okay
State

New Hampshire: The Granite State

Should be called

The Live Free or Suck My Dick State

or

The Home of Husky Women State

or

A Little Slice of Stupid State

New Jersey: The Garden State

Should be called

The Where the Bodies Are Buried State

or

The Toll Booth State

or

The Stinkiest State in the Whole USA

New Mexico: The Land of Enchantment

Should be called

> The Almost as Successful as New Coke State
>
> *or*
>
> Only Slightly Better Than the Real Mexico
>
> *or*
>
> The Abandoned Teepees and Cheap Turquoise State

New York: The Empire State

Should be called

> The Crack Whore State
>
> *or*
>
> The More Jews Than Israel State
>
> *or*
>
> The We Finance All Those Red States State

North Carolina: The Tar Heel State

Should be called

> The Could Somebody Explain What a Tar Heel Is?
> State
>
> *or*
>
> The First in Aviation, Last in Edgeecation State
>
> *or*
>
> The It Ain't Inbreedin' If They're Livestock State

North Dakota: The Peace Garden State

Should be called

The Fetal Alcohol Syndrome State

or

The South Dakota of the North

or

Not Quite Canada

Ohio: The Buckeye State

Should be called

The Mistake on the Lake

or

The Rubber Capital of America If You Don't Count Snooki's Vagina State

Oaklahomer*: The Sooner State

Should be called

The Sooner I'm Out of Here the Better State

Oregon: The Beaver State

Should be called

The Should Be Nice, Once It's Finished State

or

The Not Only Is Assisted Suicide Legal, We'll Help You Write the Note—Especially If You're from Alabama State

or

Whatever

---

* Even with the song I still can't spell the fucker.

Pennsylvania: The Keystone State

Should be called

> The Our Football Coaches Put the Man in Boys State
>
> *or*
>
> The Our Two Biggest Cities Are Shitholes State
>
> *or*
>
> The QVC State

Rhode Island: The Ocean State

Should be called

> The Less Square Miles Than Kirstie Alley's Ass State
>
> *or*
>
> The Sadly, Size Matters State

South Carolina: The Palmetto State

Should be called

> When North Carolina Just Isn't Bigoted Enough State
>
> *or*
>
> The Still 100% Jew Free, Whoopee! State
>
> *or*
>
> Jesus' Summer Home State

South Dakota: The Coyote State

Should be called

> The It's So Boring the Faces on Mount Rushmore Are
> Yawning State
>
> *or*

The Census Bureau Guy Can Count Everybody on His
Fingers State

Tennessee: The Volunteer State

Should be called

The Mississippi Without the Panache State
or
The Elvis Got Fat and Overdosed Here State
or
The Fat Mothers with Fat Daughters State
or
The Food Stamps Can Be Fun State

Texas: The Lone Star State

Should be called

The Last Person Involved with Books Was Lee Harvey
Oswald State
or
The Proud to Be Stupid State
or
The *TV Guide* Is Considered a Book State

Utah: The Beehive State

Should be called

The Creepy Polygamous State
or
The Where Black People Are Just a Concept State

Vermont: The Green Mountain State

Should be called

The Where Pancakes Are Considered a Vegetable State

or

The No-Progress Since 1776 and Proud of It State

or

The We're Really Just an Outlet Store State

or

The Birkenstock and Hairy Pits State

Virginia: The Old Dominion State

Should be called

The Even Our Skateboards Have Gun Racks State

or

The Congressional Mistresses State

or

The Half the State Is Up on Blocks State

Washington: The Evergreen State

Should be called

The Serial Killer State

or

The Body Dumpsite State

or

The I Can't Believe It's Fucking Raining *Again* State

West Virginia: The Mountain State

Should be called

The Low Birth Weight State

or

The Eyes Far Apart State

or

The Everybody Has Black Lung Disease So You Might as Well Smoke State

or

The Proud to Be #1 in Cockfighting State

Wisconsin: The Badger State

Should be called

Where Everybody Cuts the Cheese State

or

The Land of Cheese, Beer and Brett Favre's Meat

Wyoming: The Equality State

Should be called

The Brokeback State

or

The Totally Empty State

or

Why?

or

The Each Citizen Has His Own Senator State

And as for all my good friends in Washington, D.C., and Puerto Rico: You're not states, so fuck off!

SCREW MOTHER NATURE . . .

I was adopted.

■

I hate Mother Nature and I don't want to be one with her. I want to be one with room service, a complimentary breakfast and a massage from a good-looking Costa Rican boy named Hector whose concept of a happy ending should include both making an old woman happy and getting his green card at the same time.

I hate outdoorsy types. When someone says to me, "Karen's an outdoorsy gal," I take that to mean Karen's a moron who sometimes finds herself weeping uncontrollably when she's on her fourth wine cooler and a k.d. lang song comes on the radio. Or, as my mother used to say, Karen's on the cusp of lesbianism but is afraid to commit to muff-diving and cargo pants.

I hate "rustic."

Rus-tic (adjective)
1. Plain and simple
2. Of country lifestyle

You can't spell "rustic" without the word "rust," which is why "rustic furniture" is just furniture-salesman code for "stuff we found by the side of the highway." Rustic furniture is almost as bad as "distressed" furniture, which is furniture-salesman code for "stuff we salvaged from a crack house."

I hate camping. The human race has evolved for sixty billion years so we wouldn't have to do things like sleep on the ground under a canvas tarp. Why would we want to do that now? Camping is almost as stupid as doing your own dentistry at home with a pair of pliers. Camping involves sleeping bags. If a bag has a body in it the body should be wearing a toe tag and there should be a certificate of death.

The only people who should live outdoors are Pygmies, the homeless, feral retards like Nell and women who stalk married men or live in the shrubs outside their boyfriends' bedroom windows. If I want to sleep outdoors I'll pass out behind a Dumpster like Nick Nolte.

Sleeping outdoors is not a natural state for humans. Why do you think the cavemen were called *cave*men— because they had housing! Even way back when, before fire, the wheel and basic cable, the Cro-Magnon men had the common sense to seek shelter. They may have had hair on their tongues and dragged their knuckles, yet they knew enough to put a roof over their heads when they went night-night.

I hate all bugs. And don't tell me about their importance in the food chain. Everyone says, "Oh, but there are good bugs like the praying mantis that eat mosquitoes and other bugs." I hate displays of public prayer. Frankly, I find praying mantises pushy and offensive. And dollars to donuts, a good number of these praying mantises are born-again, evangelical mantises who hate the gay mantises, black mantises and Mexican mantises, which, as you know, are a huge part of my audience.

Of all the bugs, I hate flies the most. If God is so perfect and never makes mistakes then how does He explain flies? They're nothing more than public nuisances, like preachers who claim they can "pray the gay away," or Glenn Beck, or Flo from those Progressive Insurance commercials whose hairdo, by the way, tends to attract flies. Flies serve no purpose; they don't do anything. They don't make honey; they don't help farmers by cross-pollinating crops; they don't help the environment; they don't even look nice. Have you ever seen a fly, up close and personal? Flies make the Elephant Man look attractive. They have gigantic, multifaceted eyes that are twice the size of their bodies. Getting a fly fitted for contacts is a nightmare. In fact, put a fly in a cocktail gown and it's no longer an insect, it's Anne Hathaway. (Although the fly would probably do a much better job hosting the Oscars. At least a fly would create some buzz.) What I hate most about flies is that they have no idea how to vacation. They were born with the gift of flight; they could go anywhere in the world they wanted. But where do they hang out? On shit. They're like the Heidi and Spencer of the insect world.

I hate free-range chickens. Why should chickens walk free while thousands of political dissidents languish in prisons all over the world? If Nelson Mandela can handle twenty-seven years behind bars, Henny Penny can deal with being in a coop for a couple of months. I don't give a shit if the chickens are enjoying the countryside, holding each other's claws and singing, "You are the wind beneath my wings." I don't care if they lead healthy lifestyles and enjoy summer breezes by a babbling brook; I don't care if the chickens of the world are happy. I care if they taste good with creamed spinach and potatoes.

I hate forest rangers. Maybe this is psychological baggage from my childhood because as a young, impressionable girl I was very confused by Smokey the Bear. On one hand I thought, *This is great. Smokey is encouraging people to prevent forest fires.* But then I thought, *On the other hand aren't bears dangerous, predatory carnivores? Why is Smokey talking to me in those TV* *commercials? Is he really crying at the thought of a forest fire, or is he just trying to get me into his van?* As an adult I know that bears really aren't friendly, harmless creatures who talk to people about preventing forest fires. Bears are husky, hairy gay men who wear leather chaps with the asses cut out.

I hate hiking. If we were supposed to hike the Lord wouldn't have invented the taxicab. I never hike anywhere. Ever since I watched Julie Andrews drag all of those fucking kids across the alps in *The Sound of Music*, I said, "This is not for me." The lederhosen, the backpacks, the schlepping . . . Yes, Julie was saving all of those von Trapps from the Nazis, but really? I'm not standing up for the Nazis here, but did you ever actually hear those von Trapp kids sing? Talk about a crime against humanity! Could a movie be any more syrupy? I got type 2 diabetes just from listening to the sound track. How do you solve a problem like Maria? Get her laid, obviously. Besides, they weren't real Nazis, they were musical Nazis. In real life Himmler and his SS henchmen never burst into a shtetl in Vienna and began singing "Danke Schoen" in three-part harmony. I don't care how good in bed Christopher Plummer is, I ain't hiking to Switzerland. Honestly, I don't know why people hike at all. If Satan called me and said, "Joan, if you give me your firstborn, I guarantee that for the rest of eternity you'll be carried everywhere you go," I'd say, "Lucifer! I love my daughter!!! . . . Can you throw in a toaster oven or a week in Cancun?"

I hate fishing, other than for compliments.
The word "fish" is not supposed to be a verb; it's an
entrée. I'll eat salmon, but I won't wander into the river
to catch one. Don't get me wrong, I love seeing fish in
their natural habitat . . . inside the lobster tank at The
Palm. But I don't need to know how fish are caught to
enjoy my filet of sole for lunch, any more than I need
to meet seven-year-old diamond miners in Africa to
enjoy my new necklace.

**And I hate those huge rubber wading boots
you have to wear to go fishing.** They go with
nothing, including that straw game bag you're supposed to put your fish in. The only way you'll ever see
me in a pair of those is if they're a part of the new
Jimmy Choo bladder control collection.

I hate people who "swim with the dolphins"
because they saw *Flipper* when they were six and their
lives have just never been the same ever since. Swimming
with dolphins is a nightmare. One, they poop in the
water. And two, sometimes they try to mate with us!
Which wouldn't be so bad if they'd call you the next
day or send flowers. Having sex with a huge, wet, slimy
mammal who's got a functioning blowhole is a living
hell. And if you don't believe me, just ask Mrs. James
Gandolfini.

**I hate people who participate in extreme
sports** like skydiving, mountain climbing or dating

Gary Busey. If you have to wear a helmet or sign a release form to do it, it's not a sport. It's a symptom of your sick need to pretend your meaningless life isn't meaningless. I take lots of risks in my life: I was on *Celebrity Apprentice*, I've undergone plastic surgery 398 times and I routinely make fun of Kirstie Alley, who could kill me with one swipe of her paw. And speaking of laughing in the face of death, do you know I've flown Continental Airlines at least a hundred times? I don't need to jump out of planes or scale mountains to put a little zest in my life. I can get that sort of thrill any time by walking the streets of New York without a Glock in my purse.

There are a million TV movies and documentaries about thrill seekers who feel the need to climb Mount Everest. I'm not one of those people. I'm the kind of people who needs to *watch* those TV specials, but only to see the climbers either freeze to death or plunge thousands of feet off a cliff. If I ever feel the need to climb a mile-high summit I'll mount Kevin James.

I'll cut Sir Edmund Hillary some slack because he wasn't an adventurer or thrill seeker. Everyone knows he was the first person to reach the summit of Mount Everest. What most people don't know is that he only did it to get away from his wife, Lady Esther Crooker, the Duchess of Nagging.

I hate Annie Oakley. Okay, maybe *hate* is too strong a word. I don't hate her, I resent her. Yes, she was a great markswoman and could shoot a dime out of midair from ninety feet away. Color me impressed. But what were the practical applications of this ability? Was America under attack by swarms of flying dimes at the time? If Annie wanted to do something useful, why didn't she learn how to shoot pennies out of the air? Everyone hates pennies. They're useless.

Aileen Wuornos was an even better shot than Annie Oakley—she could shoot a john in the head from fifty feet while counting her cash *and* putting her stained pants back on *at the same time.* Where's *her* Broadway show?

I hate nudists, because the people most likely to waltz around naked are the last people in the world who should ever be waltzing around naked. The only people more disgusting to look at than nudists are swingers. In both cases they're giving it away for free because nobody wants to buy it. You don't see men who look like George Clooney flashing their bits on a nude beach; you see men who look like Rosemary Clooney.

I hate the Boy Scouts of America. Nothing pisses me off more than having some pimple-faced kid offer to help me cross the street. Keep your dirty mitts off me, tent boy, or I'll hit you with my walker. Boy Scouts are taught totally useless survival skills, like campfire making and whittling. Who whittles anymore? Last I heard, all of that Ozark/hillbilly craftwork had been outsourced to China and now Pappy Foo Yong whittles ashtrays and pipes for eight cents a day on a porch in Yangtze. The only good thing the Scouts do is teach the boys knot-tying skills, which will come in handy because they're all probably closet cases. I hope that someday the Boy Scouts of America get on the reality train and start giving out merit badges for fisting and nipple torture.

I hate the wilderness families on television.

Every rustic ranch family is portrayed as hardscrabble workin' folk, who believe in a day's work for a day's pay. I believe in a day's work for a month's pay, plus residuals and, if it's a feature, points. Do you remember *Bonanza*? It was about a widowed father (Lorne Greene) and his three relentlessly unmarried sons (Dan Blocker, Pernell Roberts and Michael Landon) who operated the Cartwright family cattle ranch. There were no womenfolk around, just an Asian servant named Hop Sing whose family died when Dan Blocker sat on them. The Cartwrights worked together, played together and fought together. They were America's last frontiersmen, carving a new nation out of the unforgiving earth of a vast continent. Oddly enough, Lorne Greene and Michael Landon were Jewish. Jewish cowboys? "Watch it, folks. That murderous sidewinder Tex Blickstein is comin' to town tonight with his six-shooter and his tax attorney and he's gonna want to see everybody's federal return from the past five years!"

Because *Bonanza* was such a hit, Michael Landon went on to do another show called *Little House on the Prairie* about illiterates living in piles of their own horses' shit. I hated it! Mom and Pop and all the young'uns roughin' it in a little town with a church, a barn and a store. That's right, *store*. Singular. Not stores or malls or outlets—a store. Plus, the church hadn't even been converted into a gay nightclub yet—the townspeople were still using it for worship services. Who does that?!? If I want to spend time in a little town with only one church and one store I'll go to East Hampton. *Little House* was on the air for 245 years, and every time the ratings sagged either one of the kids would go blind or Ma Ingalls would shit out another brat with a biblical name. What was really creepy was that they all lived in a one-room cabin, so whenever Ma and Pa got to feeling frisky all the kids in the family had to listen. Ma Ingalls was like the Kate Gosselin of her time, except fewer people hated Ma Ingalls's guts because they didn't have Internet back then. The only thing I liked about *Little House* was the relationship the mother had with her daughters, which, on a scale of one-to-Joan Crawford, was an eight.

Since the advent of cable and the Internet there are hundreds of shows about nature and gardening and the outdoors; in fact there are entire networks devoted to useless programming, like the Discovery Channel and the Nature Channel and *OWN*.

The only good thing about nature is that it takes its course, and in that regard human beings could learn a thing or two. When animals get old and sick they go off into the woods to die; they don't burden their families with private nursing and hospice care. When was the last time you heard a gray wolf say, "Jimmy, we're not gong to be able to send you to college because Nana can't clean her paws by herself anymore, so we're going to have to use your college tuition money to provide for an assisted living lair." If dying birds can fly to distant mountaintops to die, then certainly old people can fly in formation a lot farther than Boca Raton.

WILDLY OVERRATED
NATURAL PHENOMENA

There are a lot of natural occurrences for which there is no explanation, like the northern lights or migratory birds' travel patterns. But there are others which, while easily explained, are just not that fucking interesting.

Rainbows

Judy Garland, Kermit the Frog and Jesse Jackson may have loved rainbows for their mystical, magical qualities, but not me. When I think of a rainbow I think of a family of five driving down the highway in a storm when all of sudden the sun comes out and little Susie in the back seat yells, "Hey, everybody, look—a rainbow!" And they all look up at the pretty colors in the sky. And drive under the truck in front of them, killing four and leaving little Susie in critical yet stable condition.

Earthquakes

Seismologists say earthquakes occur when giant plates under the sea shift and create a disaster. Similar to what occurs in Las Vegas when the giant plates in Wayne Newton's mouth shift. Because I spend half my time in California, earthquakes don't really bother me. In fact, I hope that the next time there's a quake my house slides into a better neighborhood. And FYI, I hate the assholes who say, "Stand in a doorway during an earthquake; you'll be safe." Sure. And I'll hide in the pantry when they drop a hydrogen bomb.

Niagara Falls

Niagara Falls bores me; the only people who find it fascinating are honeymooners and the suicidal. If you can get a suicidal honeymooner to go, then it might be worth my making the schlep. For years daredevils used to go over Niagara Falls in a barrel or wearing flotation devices to see if they would survive the fall. The last person to survive a fall over the Horseshoe Falls part of Niagara was a forty-year-old-man named Kirk Jones, of Stupidville, USA. He went over the falls with only the clothes on his back. What a schmuck; they weren't even waterproofed.

The Grand Canyon

It's just a giant crack that has thousands of people inside of it every year. Do your own Snooki joke. (Do I have to do everything for you?)

Cows

They eat grass and produce milk. Why not challenge these biological marvels? Feed them aluminum and steel and see if they can come up with a Mercedes or a Humvee.

Rain Forests

Rain forests are essential to Earth's ecosystem, but since the only time I spend outdoors is walking from my plastic surgeon's office to the parking lot, I really don't give a shit about our global ecosystem. When I hear the words "rain forest" I think of three things: humidity, humidity, humidity. Have you ever been to the Amazon? Frizz central. Every baboon has split ends. Which, coupled with the thumbs on the feet and the purple ass, is not a good look.

I HATE SHOW BUSINESS . . .
IT'S A CRUEL MISTRESS

Due to residuals there are
dead people who actually make
more money than I do.

■

Not only is there a broken heart for every light on Broadway, but a broken cherry, too. I know; I "lost" my virginity 163 times. I spent more time on my back than Michelangelo painting the Sistine Chapel and all I've managed to do is fuck my way to the middle and end up with a vaginal canal that seats ten.

I hate that the Motion Picture Academy of Arts and Sciences calls itself the Motion Picture Academy of Arts and Sciences. Any institution, organization or body that includes Carrot Top, Gallagher and the guy from the *Jackass* movies in its membership is neither an art nor a science.

I hate that the Academy Awards ceremony calls itself "The night Hollywood honors its own." When are these fuckers not honoring their own? These people have more award ceremonies than Mia Farrow has children. Other professions don't carry on like this. When was the last time you saw a TV awards show for proctologists? "And the winner of best supporting finger is . . . Dr. Murray Weinstein, for his fine work in Marvin Schissel's ass."

I hate the SAG Awards, even though they were named for my boobs. The show always opens with some of the stars in attendance looking directly into the camera and saying, pretentiously, and with ridiculous amounts of fake gravitas, "I'm Robert De Niro and I'm an *act-or!* I'm Denzel Washington and I'm an *act-or!* I'm Christian Bale and I'm an *act-or!*" Calm the fuck down. You're actors. You're not curing cancer or solving the Middle East crisis or buying smiles for those one-toothed cleft palate kids on the back of the *Enquirer.* You pretend you're Batman. You wear tight pants and a cape and you pretend you're saving Gotham City from the Penguin. Get a grip.

I hate Christian Bale. This is nothing personal. I hate all men named Christian.

I hate the Emmy Awards ceremony. It's just an evening to honor actors who are too old, short, homely or uninsurable to work in movies anymore. I keep mine on the mantel above my fireplace.

I hate the Tony Awards show. I can't get booked anywhere that night because every gay man in the world is at the fucking Tonys.

I hate agents, managers, lawyers and publicists (except mine, of course). For those of you not familiar with show business, imagine a large, hideous vulture with wet lips and a pinkie ring circling around, picking bones. Now imagine the carcass isn't dead yet, just between projects or waiting for a green light from the network. In a nutshell, here's what these showbiz hangers-on do: Your agent is supposed to protect you from unemployment and poverty; your manager is supposed to protect you from your agent; and your lawyer is supposed to protect you from your new cellmate, because jail is where you've landed after your agent and manager fucked up. And your publicist is there to make sure that your misfortune is somehow spun properly so that even though your career is done, she'll be able to benefit from your troubles and move up the PR food chain and get really big clients, like Leonardo DiCaprio or Tom Cruise or the Taco Bell dog.

I hate actors who don't admit their age. Goldie Hawn came up to a friend of mine one day and said, "Can you believe I'm a grandmother?" The answer is: Yes! You're sixty-six fucking years old; you could be a great-grandmother. If you were Puerto Rican you could be a great-great-great-great-great-grandmother. *Laugh-In* was fifty years ago; move on.

I hate Tom Cruise. First of all, he's always smiling. No 5' 8" man, not even one who lives on a diet of Ritalin and gin, is happy like that all the time. He's always got this shit-eating grin on his face, like he just got a note from his managers telling him that Mimi Rogers and Nicole Kidman are extending their confidentiality agreements. Second, in TV interviews Tom laughs inappropriately and much too vociferously at non-humorous declarative statements, which is ironic because in real life he can't take a fucking joke at all. All you have to do is make one simple, little, harmless, innocuous aside like, "The Scientology spaceship was late today; it had to stop in Fire Island to pick up Tom Cruise," and he has a pack of lawyers at your door faster than Katie Holmes can say, "No, really, he loves me *in that way*. I swear."

I hate Nicole Kidman. She makes stupid movies like *Cold Mountain* and *The Hours*. She became an A-list actress for wearing putty on her nose. My face is made entirely of paraffin and chewing gum and that cunt wins an Oscar? Hate her.

I hate Jennifer Aniston. She keeps making the same romantic "comedy" movie over and over and over again and it's always not funny, not funny, not funny.

I hate Marlee Matlin's interpreter. I want to give him the finger.

I hate reality stars who act like they have talent. Getting punched, beaten, arrested and contracting STDs on a weekly basis is not talent, its alcoholism. (Snooki, I hope someone is reading this book to you.) I have a new reality show I'm pitching: Take Katy Perry, Justin Bieber and Dog the Bounty Hunter and his wife and put them on an island and let them fight to the death until only one is left alive. The show's called *Who Gives a Fuck?*

I especially hate *The Real Housewives of New Jersey, Atlanta* and *Orange County*. A *real* housewife is more concerned about her children than her ratings; okay maybe not more, but at least as much (unless the child is really ugly, in which case she should try to sell him on eBay and use that as a story line during sweeps). A real housewife has her plastic surgery done quickly and quietly and would never be seen in public until her Donald Duck lips have settled down and the scars have either faded or been pushed so far behind her ears that you can only see them in a rearview mirror. *The Real Housewives of Beverly Hills* know all of this—which is why I don't hate them as much. Plus, one of them was smart enough to possibly have a gay husband with financial troubles who killed himself in the middle of the season; that's my kind of gal.

I hate Hollywood fads, especially yoga. If I want to see a downward facing dog I'll push Betty Friedan off of a chair. I picked Betty Friedan because

(a) she's homely and (b) she's dead. If I make that joke about a homely woman who's still alive, NOW, NARAL, the ACLU and the LPGA will all tell me, "FU."

I hate Pilates, Rolfing, Spinning and est and I don't need them. They involve twisting, turning and peeing. I do all that in bed every night now.

I hate night tennis. The only people who really like hitting balls at night are debutantes and Nathan Lane.

I hate all of the fad diets, like the grapefruit diet or the cookie diet or the Beverly Hills diet where you only eat fruit and you shit seeds. Or the Scarsdale Diet, where you lose weight because you only eat prison food because you killed your diet doctor. I hate the meat diet where you swallow meat five times a day. It's very popular in West Hollywood. I think the most effective diet is the Jersey Shore diet where you only eat foods you can spell. Those kids haven't seen an egg in twelve years.

I hate celebrities that get paid to lose weight almost as much as I hate not being one of them. Jenny Craig probably gave Valerie Bertinelli hundreds of thousands of dollars to eat *their* food and drop twenty pounds over the course of a year. If they would have given me the money they could have kept their goddamned food and I'd have gone to Auschwitz for a week and dropped fifty.

I hate Scientology. Their spaceships don't offer frequent-flyer plans, and when you travel as much as I do you're always looking to build up miles or earn points or get coupons for an upgrade. I can forgive that they believe aliens come down and bring you to another planet, but flying to that other planet in coach? Not *pour moi*. John Travolta and Kirstie Alley are big Scientologists—and I mean big. I could never join them because I don't do fattening.

I hate Kabbalah. Call me stupid but I'm not going to use Madonna as a travel agent on my spiritual journey. Quite frankly I'm not going to use Madonna as a guide for anything. I just saw her movie, *W.E.* It s.u.c.k.e.d. And I'm not going to wear a red string as an accessory unless it's made by Yves Saint Laurent.

I hate Deepak Chopra. He's written the same fucking book thirty-five times and these dopes who buy them still can't find their inner serenity. Want some peace and quiet? Save your money on Deepak's books and slip your kids a couple of Xanax and put them in the closet.

I hate showbiz restaurants that have caricatures of their famous customers on the walls. You're supposed to be proud that your chin goes into the next picture? I've had so much work done restaurants have two caricatures of me: "before" and "before that."

I hate "in" restaurants that are hot for a minute. I really hate that they let you know how hot *you* are by where you sit. You go to the right or the left like Sophie's Choice. Jane Seymour's knuckles are rawer than the steak tartare from hanging on to the leg of the table. "I'm not going left in Spago . . . noooo!!!!"

I hate it when I can't get into trendy, phony, pretentious restaurants. "There's a three-month wait, Miss Rivers. Sorry!" And then some scrawny, anorexic party girl with no underwear walks right in. "Who is that?" "Oh, she was in *Mean Girls*!"

What the fuck is *Mean Girls*? No matter whose name you mention, she was in *Mean Girls* and I couldn't pick her out of a police lineup if my life depended on it. If I find out that Judi Dench and Helen Mirren were in *Mean Girls* I'm going to go out and buy an AK-47 and hunt my agent down.

I hate spending three weeks trying to get a reservation for four months later and by the time July rolls around the place has closed and become a rehab center. Do you remember the Fashion Café? It was a hot spot owned by Hollywood supermodels that lasted for a week and a half. What a good idea. A restaurant run by bulimics. They didn't have a tasting menu, they had a purging menu. The place only had six tables but thirty-two stalls. Their special of the day was Imodium. Their slogan was "Bring a friend! Second guest pukes for free."

I think I've found a way to get into these places: Stand right behind Betty White. You've got a fifty-fifty shot at a good seat, especially if she's got a cough.

I hate Hollywood fund-raisers. I am so bored going to a twenty-five million dollar house to hear a mogul say, "Good news, everyone. Tonight we've raised almost twelve thousand dollars!" You paid your gay hustler more than that, you cheap thing. Why not spare all of us the canapés, small talk and crème brûlée and just write a damn check?

I hate new millionaires who are investing in art and have an original Marc Chagall hanging over the sofa—right next to a velvet Elvis and a painting of dogs playing poker. If the only taste you have is in your mouth then invest in something no one will see . . . like a late-night talk show on Fox.

I hate Hollywood's lists: the A-list, the B-list and the D-list. The only list I like is *Schindler's List* and that's only because I'm sucking up to Steven Spielberg, aggressively looking for film work so I don't have to break my ass writing another book.

I hate that all the stars in Hollywood smoke. It's not smog, it's Lindsay Lohan. I drove past MTV; there was a white cloud of smoke over the studio. I thought they were electing a pope.

I hate that everyone in Hollywood has a sex tape . . . except me. Maybe it's time for me to do something groundbreaking: nana-porn. I'll call it, *I Am Curious (Why My Diaper Is Yellow).*

I hate the actors who stay in New York instead of going to Hollywood because they are "artists" and don't want to "compromise their craft." Now the only "kraft" they have is the macaroni and cheese they eat for dinner six nights a week. "Theater actor" is an old English word that means "cater waiter."

I hate gypsies, the itinerant Broadway dancers who've been twirling and plié-ing for thirty years and are still hopeful and eager and waiting for their big break, gosh darn it! The only break they're going to get is their spine, when their flat feet and thick ankles collapse from standing on food-stamp lines since 1977.

I hate stage actors who take thirty-six curtain calls at the end of a play. I think actors who keep taking bows at the end of the play should have to stay in character. At the end of *The Miracle Worker* Helen Keller should walk off the stage and fall into the orchestra pit; at the end of *Death of a Salesman* Willy Loman should blow his head off in the lobby; and at the end of *Cats* the actors should have to lick themselves and cough up fur balls.

When I finish a play, I come out, bow and go back to my dressing room to have sex with a stagehand—assuming I can find a straight one. I don't need the audience validation to make me feel complete; I need a quickie.

MY FAVORITE FAMOUS COUPLES

Woody and Soon Yi

Only in Appalachia would a father-daughter marriage be considered normal. And even then that's only in the bad parts of Appalachia. Even cousin-fuckers have standards. What I think about is before Woody proposed to Soon Yi, did he ask himself for her hand in marriage?

Donny and Marie

Who am I to throw stones? Whatever it is, it's working. He's a little bit country, and she's still a little bit postpartum.

Bonnie and Clyde

If not for the pilfering and the anger management issues, they might've been the perfect couple. However, Clyde sometimes had a little trouble getting his pistol to fire.

Napoleon and Josephine

Other than the fact that he liked to keep his hands to himself, they had a great sex life. Josephine's safe word was "Waterloo."

Diego Rivera and Frida Kahlo

They had art, they had passion, they had eyebrows . . . Thank God they didn't have children. *Rrr-uuffff!*

Elvis and Priscilla Presley

To this day, every time I see Priscilla Presley all can I think is, "Those are the lips that sucked the cock of the King of Rock 'n' Roll." I hated seeing a young attractive person turn into such a bloated zombie. And what happened to Elvis was not so nice, either.

Elizabeth Taylor Hilton Wilding Todd Fisher Burton Burton Warner and Larry Fortensky

She had no choice but to marry Larry. She'd already married everyone else. What people don't realize is that Liz spent most of her fortune on monogramming.

Bill Clinton and Monica Lewinsky

They'd still be together if she'd found a one-hour dry cleaner. She gave size twenty-eights hope for a future in the Oval Office . . . at least under the desk.

Scarlett O'Hara and Rhett Butler

He was unfaithful and nasty and she was a nag and a liar. They would have fit in very nicely with my family.

Laverne and Shirley

I'm not saying they were lesbians. I'm saying they should have been. "Schlemiel. Schlmazel. Muff divers, incorporated."

Lucy and Desi

Everyone loved Lucy. Including Desi. He just loved coochie more.

Pierre and Marie Curie

They were truly the world's first nuclear family. He married her because she had that certain glow. And they had a beautiful wedding, even if the photos were all in black and white.

Michael Jackson and Bubbles the Chimp

It didn't work out between Michael and Bubbles because only Michael wanted children. Boy, oh boy, did he want children. Mostly boys.

Streisand and Redford in *The Way We Were*

Unless was he was suffering from a case of hysterical blindness, I still don't buy it.

Heinz Adolf Hitler and His Tomato, Eva Braun

Eva: Dolf, mein pumpschky, where are we going on our
    honeymoon?

Adolf: To heaven, mein little wienerschnitzel baby.

Eva : What are we doing after the ceremony?

Adolf: Afterward the Goehrings are coming over with a can
    of gasoline and, man, are we going to get lit.

Eva: Oh, Adolf, I am so happy. If I died right here and now,
    I would die a happy woman.

Adolf: You know mein anti-Semitic minx, it's funny that you
    should say that.

Heinz and *His* Tomato

They built an empire together. Now *that's* romance.

PEOPLE

My uncle Leonard used to proudly tell everyone that he was a "people person."

My uncle Leonard was a coroner.

■

I hate "people persons." They have no sense of self-awareness. They think they're peppy and fun and oodles of laughs and that everyone at the party is thrilled when they walk in the door grinning and chirping. In reality, everyone is trying to get out of the room as if there were mustard gas leaking through the vents. These people are not peppy and fun and oodles of laughs. They're overbearing, obnoxious and energy-draining fucks.

I hate people who complain that "Joan says 'fuck' too much." I say "them" a lot more than I say "fuck," and they don't complain about that. So fuck them.

"Can't you just say 'the f-word' instead?" What are we, six? We're speaking to each other in code now like parents talking about daddy's drinking in front of junior? *Fuck* is one of the most commonly used words in the English language and that's a fucking fact. People could be just as disturbed about the word "hemorrhoid" but they aren't. You don't see anyone calling it the "h-word." As far as I'm concerned, people who call *fuck* the "f-word" are a-holes.

I hate people who describe dessert as "decadent." Getting fingered by a nun is decadent. Chocolate simply tastes good.

I hate people who pronounce Hitler's name "Ah-dolf" instead of "Ay-dolf." That ruins the entire Holocaust experience for me.

I hate the counter workers at fast-food restaurants who use microphones to place orders with the kid working the French fry machine. For starters, pimply Pete is five feet away from you, not five miles. Secondly, you're not introducing U2 at Wembley Stadium at a benefit for the hungry kids in Africa; you're in a Wendy's ordering onion rings for a fat caregiver named T'anisha.

I hate people who yell at the people who work at fast-food restaurants. If something goes wrong with an order they scream, "What are you, an idiot?" Of course he's an idiot. He's a forty-seven-year-old man making a dollar fifty an hour and wearing a paper hat. What are you yelling at him for? The guy works at a fast-food place. Acting like an idiot is part of his job description. The help-wanted ad for that job reads: "Must know how to act like an idiot. Mammals preferred." And don't make him cry by asking him how much a Quarter Pounder weighs.

I hate people who stand in front of me on a long line at Burger King and when they finally get to the counter to order they have no idea what they want to order. Asshole, you've been standing there for twenty-five minutes with nothing to do but study the menu. Your head is emptier than Tony Bennett's balls.

I hate people who bring a bottle of water into a job interview. If you need to be hydrated that badly you're not going to get the job because no business wants to take on a health risk who becomes parched by having to answer simple questions like, "Where did you work before this?" or "How long have you been on Megan's List?"

I hate those pretentious assholes who insist on being referred to as "doctor" even though they are only Ph.D.s. You want to be a doctor? Go to medical school. You're not qualified to stick a finger up my ass just because you read Chaucer.

I hate people who say they're "workaholics."
There is no such thing. Hitler put in a lot of hours.
Would you call him a workaholic? People who work
24/7 are not "addicted" to work…they either hate their
families or don't have basic cable. My AA friends say
that addicts are powerless over their addictions. I can
see being unable to quit drinking or smoking or doing
drugs. But working? I guarantee you that not one person in the world was ever found dead in a pool of vomit
in an alley because they couldn't stop spackling or putting up drywall.

**I hate people who refer to their field of study
as a discipline.** You want discipline? Put a ball gag
in your mouth and tell Mommy you've been naughty.
Now shut up and do your homework before I have to
spank you and send your wife a note telling her you've
been a bad boy.

**I hate people who don't make eye contact
when they talk**—especially during sex in the mis-
sionary position. I mean what am I paying for here anyway? And I really hate people who make eye contact
but only with one eye. I hate people who have a lazy
eye, where one eye is reading the paper and the other
is drifting around their head to take a look behind
them. And I really, really hate people who have one
glass eye and don't tell you; they just leave it up to you
to figure it out. This ruined my friendship with Sandy
Duncan.

I hate women who feel compelled to have vaginal reconstructive surgery "for their man." Just because your lips are loose and your vagina's become a small cabin, why should you have to slice and dice your moneymaker? I say: Let him get a bigger dick.

I hate that I'm the only woman in show business who wasn't sexually abused by a father, uncle or neighbor. Roseanne, Janice Dickinson, Mackenzie Phillips, all of them were diddled by a relative, but not me. Why? What am I, a piece of shit? "Don't you like my new perfume, Uncle Marvin? It's by Fisher-Price. I have feelings, just none below the waist." Maybe I wasn't pretty enough or I wasn't Daddy's type. . . . Look, I don't want to brag, but I can toss my hair to and fro, and really throw it down in a bedroom. His loss.

I hate giants. Why should I have to carry gauze and plasma in my purse because you keep banging your head on the doorway? Inordinately tall people are a huge pain in the ass. Just ask the twenty thousand women Wilt Chamberlain banged.

I hate people who think it's cute to say to a giant, "How's the weather up there?" I hope he says, "Raining," and spits on them. Just because someone's a genetic anomaly doesn't give you the right make cruel, hurtful remarks to him or her. Unless they're dwarves, in which case anything goes.

I hate people who use clichés and then smirk as though they've said something original, or as some of you may know them, cruise ship comics. There is no time or place for spewing out endless streams of trite, hackneyed, recycled verbiage. These people are as funny as a rubber crutch.

I hate people who like modern art. "Isn't this white on white fabulous?" Dude, we're in an art supply store. That's just a blank canvas. "Maybe, but I still find it powerful."

"Joan, what do you think the artist is trying to say?" He's not *trying* to say anything; he is saying something. What he's saying is, "I can't believe some jackass is going to pay a million dollars for this piece of shit."

I hate guests who expect you to take care of them at a dinner party. What would you like to drink? "Oh, anything you bring me will be fine." Really? Okay, how about a glass of Wite-Out or a gallon of Sherwin-Williams latex house paint? Maybe a dusty coral or hunter green?

I hate men who try to pass off syphilis as jock itch. I know the difference; I've had both And no, Newt Gingrich, I'm not just singling you out.

I hate people who stick their gum under the bottom of their seat in movie theaters. Don't they know that space is reserved for boogers and snot?

I hate people who think Jesus is perfect. The man came back from the dead; okay, impressive, even David Copperfield never pulled that one off. But why would a perfect man host a big dinner for his best friends and then only serve them bread? And would it have killed him to e-mail saying: I'm on my way? Nothing, not a word, he just shows up at the door. Additionally, his appalling lack of manners doesn't speak very well of his father's parenting skills. Let's hope he gets such rudeness from his mother's side of the family.

I hate lesbians who "appreciate" jokes instead of laughing at them. My timing isn't based on your "appreciation." I need you to laugh, butcherella, so yank your head out of that carpet sample and give it up. My sisters of Sappho friends also need to learn that every punch line doesn't have to involve politics, animal rights or Melissa Etheridge. Also, a little fashion hint: When you're going to be out in public, shave your legs and pits. This isn't Europe, and the lumberjack look didn't work for Paul Bunyan and it's not going to work for you.

I hate fat ethnic girls who wear "LET'S GET NAKED" T-shirts six sizes too small. I don't want to hear from you, let alone your clothing, and I *reeeaaalllyyy* don't want to see you naked. Here's a thought, Jenny from the block, how about a T-shirt that fits you right and says, "LET'S GET A JOB!" As you know, I have little sympathy for the blind, but I'd rather gouge my eyes out with a hot poker than look at porcine Paulina's protruding pudenda.

I hate people who, in the course of conversation actually use the words "asbestos," "beverage," "*ciao,*" "*shalom*" or "*hola.*"

I hate people who try to sound smart by using words they don't know. This is the height of superfluous vicissitude.

I hate people who fail at suicide attempts; talk about losers. If you can't even kill yourself what good are you to the rest of us? If you're so depressed that you really don't want to be here, then try a surefire method of offing yourself. Jump under a train or hop off a bridge or date Sammy the Bull. None of this "*Weeelllll,* I took some pills" shit. I say man up and learn to pull the trigger with your toe.

I hate clueless housewives, and not just the ones in New York, Atlanta, New Jersey, Beverly Hills and Orange County. I mean the ones like John Wayne Gacy's wife. When a dog sniffs a fire hydrant he knows everything about every dog that ever peed there. Yet Gacy had twenty boys buried in the crawl space under the house and Mrs. G. had no idea. She never noticed that boyish smell in the air ducts or the five hundred bags of lime in the pantry, right next to the Special K, or the collection of Boy Scout uniforms he had in his sock drawer. Clueless.

I hate psychiatrists who say, "Jack's suicide attempt wasn't real; it was just a cry for help." If you want to hear a cry for help get an iPhone. Please don't turn your need for attention into something I have to mop up in the bathroom. I don't want to hear a cry for help; I want to hear a widow shrieking.

I hate state-fair people. I've never seen a fatter group of people in my life. Although maybe I shouldn't say, "fatter group of people." It's pejorative. Perhaps I should go with "herd of humanity." I was recently a judge at the Nevada state fair and I couldn't tell the livestock from the customers. I mistakenly pinned the blue ribbon for best heifer on a fifty-two-year-old soccer mom from Carson City. She got so mad at me she actually left the salt lick long enough to throw a shoe and cough up a bale of hay.

I hate people who are happy for other people. It's unnatural, like polygamy or bestiality or cotton/poly blends. There are two kinds of people in this category: people who are genuinely happy for others, and people who pretend to be genuinely happy for others. People who are genuinely happy for others are usually Mormons or retards. People who pretend to be genuinely happy for others are usually agents or managers.

I hate the Holocaust survivor who can't stop talking about how terrible it was that all she had to eat for an entire month was a piece of bread and yet she still managed to live. She was on the Dr. Mengele method. I'm so jealous of her. She got a free, full treatment and didn't have to pay those outrageous spa fees.

I hate police officers who don't recognize me when they pull me over. Let's say I missed a stop sign or forgot to signal or ran over a toddler in a cross-walk. Hey, I'm sorry about that and I promise I'll pay more attention next time, but the least the cop could do is recognize me and squeal, "Oh, my God, it's Joan Rivers! Miss Rivers, would mind signing, here? Not the citation, my autograph book . . . And would it be okay if we scraped Timmy off your grille so you can get to your sold-out concert tonight? And I won't even put any points on your license because Timmy is . . . I mean, was, a bratty kid."

I hate narcissists. They never talk about me.

I hate people who don't know how to milk a disease for all it's worth. Everyone knows how to play the cancer card, but why not learn how to make the most out of lesser illnesses? Let's say you don't feel like going to your horrible niece Jennifer's bat mitzvah because she's a whiny sourpuss who likes to have sex with illegal immigrants. A well-publicized bout of irri-table bowel syndrome should get you out of that charming family occasion. When they mail you the menu card that says, "Chicken or Fish," just write, "Wa-ter and soda crackers. My flatulence is not under control." And anorexia nervosa is a great excuse because nobody but nobody wants to be sitting near Skeletor when she collapses in a heap—ask Ashton Kutcher. And hives serves as a surefire excuse to not lend a hand because, not only are the welts horrific looking, you can make sure they know they're contagious.

I hate people who try to one up you when discussing tragedies. "My husband died in Tower One on 9/11." "You think that's bad? We had reservations at Windows on the World that night. It was horrible; we had to eat in." "My daughter was just diagnosed with juvenile diabetes; she'll have to be in treatment for the rest of her life." "Did you know that my conjoined twins were just separated but because we didn't have insurance we had to separate them with a spatula? One didn't make it but since they were identical we don't know which one."

I hate famous stroke victims who don't realize it's time to get out of the public eye. Case in point, Kirk Douglas or Dick Clark. Who wants to see Spartacus dragging a foot or hear Dick Clark counting down New Year's, "fiy faaww fwee doo wum"? If I want to see stroke victims on TV, I'll produce a show called *Drooling with the Stars.*

I hate supermarket cashiers who carefully examine fifty-dollar bills to make sure they're not fakes. Let me get this straight: Vonette is a junior high school dropout with a drug habit and a sloped forehead, yet suddenly she's a trained expert in the exciting field of counterfeiting?

I hate people who have little teeth and giant gums, like my neighbor in apartment 8C. She has eight inches of pink gums and then tiny ivory pegs at the bottom. Her smile looks like an elephant's foot. Even worse, she's *always* smiling. She comes down the hall with this giant grin, "Hi, Joan. Hi, Joan." I look around for Sabu or the Ringling Brothers. She's the one person in the world who should be depressed and she's happier than Melissa McCarthy at an all-you-can-eat buffet.

I hate people who expect me to put a positive spin on things. It's just not me—I've tried. A hirsute, toothless woman once came backstage to meet me after a show. She said, "Joan, I'm a big fan of yours." I tried to be Penny Positive so I said, "Who needs teeth? Just think, what you save on toothpaste you can spend on electrolysis, which you need desperately!"

I hate copycat killers. Stealing another maniac's MO is not only wrong, it's lazy. If you have the time and wherewithal to take out a family of five, then you can certainly work a little harder and create your own signature MO. I know, I know, "There are no new ideas and everything's already been done, blah blah blah. . . ." I disagree. Putting body parts in a bag or a severed head in the freezer have been done to death.

Why not attempt a variation on the theme? After you decapitate somebody, rather than cluttering up the Frigidaire, why not hide the head in a toaster cozy so the grieving survivors can at least play America's new party game, "Has Anyone Seen Grandpa?"

Charles Manson was one of a kind! Ted Bundy? Classic. Aileen Wournos? Can you name another female serial killer? Be original! Leave a funny hat at the crime scene or put your victims in a bathtub full of homemade borscht, or if there are two murder victims side by side put an "I'm with stupid'" T-shirt on one of them, or, best of all, switch out the heads so when the CSIs say, "She has her mother's eyes," they're not kidding.

I hate nose pickers who are unprepared. If you have allergies or sinus problems or suffer nasal dryness then for God's sake carry a handkerchief or Kleenex or, during cold and flu season, industrial-strength wipes. Others don't need to vomit because you have a finger full of snot. When Sir Isaac Newton said, "For every action there is an equal and opposite reaction," he must've been at a stoplight and saw the guy in the car next to him picking his nose, and then threw up all over his rented Buick LeSabre.

I hate women who play coy forty years too late. Batting your eyes at a rich, handsome man or glancing at him over your shoulder like Rita Hayworth in *Gilda* is fine when you're twenty-five and in heat. But when you're sixty-five and in Huggies, it's pathetic.

I hate having to be patient with people who have early onset Alzheimer's. It's exhausting. How many times can I say, "Yes, we ate lunch already, Ruthie," or "No, it's me, Joan. Uncle Bernie's been dead since 1964." I find it much easier to simply agree with whatever it is they're doing or saying. If I walk into the room and Doris Dementia thinks I'm Marvin Gaye, I'll play right along and croon a quick chorus of "Sexual Healing" and then fuck a white woman. It's so much easier than explaining that I'm not a man, I'm not black, I'm not dead and I can't sing.

I hate whistlers. Whistling is not an art form or a music genre, it's an annoyance. You know the only person who enjoys whistling? The Whistler. I even hated it on *The Andy Griffith Show*, when Andy and Opie are going fishing or digging a shallow grave. In the 1944 film *To Have and Have Not*, Lauren Bacall says to Humphrey Bogart, "You know how to whistle, don't ya? You just put your lips together and blow." Obviously she knew how to blow because a few days later she and Bogie got engaged and married. And in 1957, Bogie blew his last breath. Maybe he should have saved his strength and stopped whistling—who knows, he might still be alive and blowing today.

I hate Whistler's mother. Whistler spent all that time studying art—he went from pencils to ink to Cray-Pas to oil to acrylics. He studied brushstrokes and depth and proportion and then, after all those years of schooling, when it came time to pose, this bitch couldn't be bothered to smile. That's one lazy mother.

I hate Mona Lisa, another arrogant supermodel doing us favor by just showing up. This ungrateful shrew sat for the great artist, Leonardo da Vinci, yet just like Whistler's mother, she found it beneath her to put on a happy face for the historic session. She just sat there, grumbling, with a sour, put-upon look on her puss. Come on—you're about to become the most popular art image in history. Generations upon generations will wait hours to stand before your image in the Louvre and whisper in awe, "I thought it would be bigger." Art historians describe Mona Lisa's smile as "enigmatic." I call it "cunty." And in spite of the fact that Mona Lisa is a dour sad sack, she is beautifully hung in the Louvre. Ironically, the statue of David is not nearly as well hung.

I hate gays who pretend they're straight and expect me to pretend along with them. If you have ball marks on your chin, don't expect me not to say anything or act as though you got them in a freak golf accident.

I hate interracial couples who pretend not to notice that they're different races. If I throw a fabulous white party in the Hamptons and one guest shows up wearing black, I'll notice. And I assure you I'll say something. I wouldn't say anything like, "So, is your family horrified?" or "Have you been cut out of the will?" No, I'll say something subtle but on point, like, "That jacket will look beautiful during Kwanzaa, no?" Or "Didn't I see you in a film with Kim Kardashian?"

Lastly, I hate people who write a book and talk about its "arc" and have a real ending. I'm out of ideas so this is all you're going to get. This is it. If you want more, wait for the paperback. It's in my contract that I have to add more pages. (Oh yeah? Let's see if they can catch me.)

ACKNOWLEDGMENTS

My lawyers have advised me that it's a good idea if not to acknowledge, then at least to express a shred of gratitude that this book has been published and will hopefully sell a million copies so I can send my grandson to college so he doesn't have to do button work in a sweatshop for a dollar-eighty a week (less taxes, kickbacks and money for smokes).

So, as per counsel: I'm grateful to all of you who helped with this book and you know who you are . . . because I certainly don't. What I am grateful about is that the people of the world are getting dumber and stupider and ruder and louder and sloppier and whorier because it gives me a whole new generation of idiots to hate. And I'm grateful that I'm in good health so that in ten years I can write a sequel to this shitty book that will sell another million copies so I can put my grandson through rehab, or at least post his bail.